The Real Estate Journey

THE REAL ESTATE JOURNEY

From Dreaming and Home Buying To Realty and Entrepreneurship

DR. BRIAN P. SIMON

NEW YORK

LONDON • NASHVILLE • MELBOURNE • VANCOUVER

The Real Estate Journey
From Dreaming and Home Buying to Realty and Entrepreneurship

Published in New York, New York, by Morgan James Publishing. Morgan James is a trademark of Morgan James, LLC. www.MorganJamesPublishing.com

Reference to scripture on page 92: Scripture marked ESV is taken from the Holy Bible, English Standard Version, copyright © 2001 by Crossway Bibles, a publishing ministry of Good News Publishers.

Reference to scripture on page 117: Unless otherwise noted, Scripture is taken from the Holy Bible, New International Version®, NIV® copyright ©1973, 1978, 1984, 2011 by Biblica, Inc.® Used by permission. All rights reserved worldwide.

ISBN 9781642793628 paperback
ISBN 9781642793635 eBook
Library of Congress Control Number: 2018913705

Cover Design by:
Ethel Daito Delacruz & Christopher Kirk

Interior Design by:
Chris Treccani
www.3dogcreative.net

Morgan James is a proud partner of Habitat for Humanity Peninsula and Greater Williamsburg. Partners in building since 2006.

Get involved today! Visit
MorganJamesPublishing.com/giving-back

ACKNOWLEDGMENTS

To my wife, Jami, and my children, Ethan and Ella: Having a husband and dad as an entrepreneur has its own special challenges. Thank you for embracing this life in the most positive way. I am so proud that you not only support me, but that you also participate in this life I chose.

To my father, mother, and sister: I am fortunate and blessed to have been raised in such a loving home.

To my West Virginia cousins, high school friends, college friends, and church community of my youth: I will always be thankful for your investment in my life.

To my church: I am thankful for my re-entrance into a caring, accepting, and talent-filled church after a ten-year absence from consistently attending any local church. Riverbend opened its doors just down the road from my home and has been tremendously positive in giving me that extra strength I will need for this next, I am sure challenging, season of my journey.

To my Virginia community: As I left the hills of West Virginia in 2001 and moved to Hampton Roads, Virginia, 17 years later I can truly say that my expectations have been greatly exceeded. This is largely due to my group of friends and their amazing children whom we have referred to as "the cluster" over the years. Raising our children, loving our spouses, and learning from one another's successes and failures has been and continues to be a true joy.

To my hard-working staff, administrators, technology team, agents, and friends who have helped our family of companies stay on the forefront of technology, thought, and execution of many strategic goals over the years: Each one of you has positively shaped aspects of our accomplished goals and vision. Special thanks to Mandy Bauswell, my editor, social media assistant, cheerleader and now PR Assistant. Thank you for your belief in me and your friendship with my wife.

To the thousands of clients we have served over the years: Thank you for choosing us. It was an honor to serve you and help make your dreams come true.

To my lifelong friend, a military hero and one of my personal heroes, Dr. John Garvin: Thank you for reigniting my desire to publish a book and speak into the lives of others outside of my own family and companies. This book would not have been born without your push.

Finally, to the Morgan James Publishing team: Special thanks to David Hancock, CEO & Founder for believing in me and my message. To my Author Relations Manager, Bonnie

Rauch, thanks for making the process seamless and easy. Many more thanks to everyone else, but especially Jim Howard, Bethany Marshall, and Nickcole Watkins.

CONTENTS

INTRODUCTION

They say that, with a handful of pretty good decisions, your forties and fifties are your most productive, fruitful, and fulfilling years, both financially and personally. Having recently entered my forties, only time will tell if that statement is true for me. Have I peaked or have I only just begun my journey? Now, on to you: Where are you in your season of life? Where do you hope to be in the next season? Here's a little piece of my story as I see it to date. I hope this book makes a positive impact on your life and those around you.

As I began to walk into my forties, I more holistically embraced that I'm an instinctively, sometimes overly excitable, serial entrepreneur. I find myself continually craving a new adventure to take money and turn it into more money, to take a system and make it larger and expandable, to take a nonprofit and give the leader a hundred ideas on how to grow it, or to try a local product or service and see how it could go national online.

Many years ago, in my early twenties, I accepted the reality that people had constant problems, and if I could solve those problems I would get paid and others would appreciate having their problems solved. Plumbers solve plumbing problems; car salespeople solve car problems; nail technicians solve finger and toenail problems; military men and women solve war and peace problems; real estate agents solve home buying, selling, and rental problems. I later learned that if you solve problems but don't have time to keep solving them, you can hire someone else to do it. That's how a business system perpetuates itself: solve a commonly experienced problem, empower leaders and managers to solve that problem, and then pick a new problem to solve. I love solving problems. I also get bored easily, which leads me on a continual journey to find new problems to solve. The key I learned a long time ago was that if you solve small in regards to financial-worth problems, you get small financial rewards/pay for solving those problems. You might be surprised and find it amusing to hear what types of problems I've solved for pay throughout my journey.

I was born and raised in a small town in Nutter Fort, West Virginia. I first realized my entrepreneurial affinities in my own home. Growing up, earning and losing money seemed to be a part of how I was taught since my father, Paul, is naturally business-minded. In reflection, my parents rarely, if ever, discouraged my various attempts to create money, sell, trade, or work deals. They would more often than not get their hands dirty, give me a ride here or there, or come and try to bail me out when I would get into a situation. For instance, I was a newspaper delivery boy. It was a great job, and I always will remember that, although it was my job, my mom, Kathy, would sometimes drive me on my route on those big Sunday mornings walking Maryland avenue, the road that was straight uphill behind my house. When I was a little older, my dad would give me projects and pay me fairly for them. He'd leave me with a jackhammer all day and point to a pad of cement and say, "I will come by with lunch." The jackhammer was about my size, but I seemed to make progress, and he was generally pleased with my work.

My parents were usually very supportive of my various entrepreneurial attempts as a kid. At one point, I tried raising fishing worms to sell. My father helped me work a deal for the used coffee grinds from the Sunday church service. I was able to create a huge worm farm, but reproduction was a big problem for me. Essentially, my worm farm never fed more than my own fishing habit.

I also sold minnows from the creek in my backyard to a local bait and tackle store down the road. I was in the creek all the time anyway, so it seemed natural when I saw the need. I'd hunt carp with a spear and catch big catfish out of broken old pipes. I knew fishing spots miles up and down the creek behind my home. My father allowed me full access to his johnboat, and I would drag it in and out almost daily for my exploits. When friends or cousins came over, I would excitedly bring them along on my adventures. It was a great source of energy and life for me. Even if no one was around, I was happy to go on my own, all day.

Another business venture began when one of my buddies and I found a ton of old bottles in the creek. We cleaned them and prepared them for a person who buys and sells things like that. We scrubbed them day after day and made them as clean as we could. We opened the phonebook and called various local businesses and invited them to drive by the house, since our thirteen-year-old selves couldn't drive yet. They would come by and offer us money if they wanted any of the old things we scavenged. It didn't last long. Turns out, the supply and demand for these antiques was not super high in Nutter Fort in the 1980s.

In my early teens, I trapped muskrats in the creek behind my house. After seeking wisdom from older locals on how to prepare the furs, and a lot of trial and error, I learned to skin them, salt their skins, and stretch them on a board. It was a very rewarding experience, as it was something new and very different. By the time I gathered enough furs, I was only able to sell a few, and then the fur market took a hit and knocked the money-making right off the table. In order to redeem my already skinned animals, I tried making my own fur gun slings and things for around the house. Ultimately, the fur market tanked, and so did my muskrat fur sales company. My wealth in muskrat fur never evolved. I was really disappointed when I found out, but I moved on. Fortunately, I was still under the age of 14. I had a roof over my head and food in the fridge, and the money was more because my dad had taught me that I should probably care about that type of thing if I planned to grow up and possibly have a family and pay bills.

Living in a small, rural, and safe neighborhood, grass-cutting and deck washing were always my number one go-tos.

I found a few flyers would keep me busy and making money all summer. As a young man, I had a huge heart and love for elderly people, whether it was my dear Aunt Rose or my grandmother, Mary, or the various elderly people I got to know on my paper route. Grass-cutting and deck cleaning were win-win jobs. I felt reward from the hugs and the appreciation for the help, as well as piling up those twenty-dollar bills to get ready for college, gas, or a hot date.

There were times I took "real" jobs, not just businesses I started on my own. One of my earliest jobs was as a waiter at Eat'n Park. I made about $5.50 per hour plus tips, which, if I sweetened up the old ladies, I could pull in some five and ten-dollar tips here and there. It was a decent job, but it mostly sharpened my skills and taught me to be bold enough to ask questions in public. I was also a lifeguard at a country club for a couple of summers. That job paid about twelve dollars per hour and I could order a free meal, which was great for a hungry lifeguard who was happy to not be cutting grass exclusively for a summer. However, I certainly kept my best grass-cutting clients, like my parents' apartments and some higher paid, big hill-type jobs to help with the cash flow.

During the middle of my sophomore year of college, I joined YWAM (Youth With A Mission). That six months made a huge impact on my life. I spent four months in Montana, two months in Venezuela, and a few weeks in Canada. While there, we all had to take a job. It was not paid, but it was required. I worked in the cafeteria. I learned to find joy in each cafeteria job, including scrubbing, cleaning, serving, or whatever got thrown at me. Working for no pay while trying to find joy in the work of my hands was a great challenge thrown at me, and I enjoyed it.

When I came home from YWAM, I was fully in love with helping people, and I was inspired to impact the world and make a difference. I believed I had found information of great value inside the Bible and that it had the power to change lives. I wanted to be a traveling idea sales person, otherwise known as a preacher. That led me to where I served as a youth pastor for a couple of years for very, very low pay, and I was happy to do it. In retrospect, working for the two great churches that I did as a youth pastor was as significant to me as it was for the students who attended and were involved. I worked so hard to pray and prepare for the gatherings, plan events, get the teens into a van, and take them on trips. I was often scared as a young man myself, but I just kept pressing forward. I was a youth pastor who loved investing in the leaders in my group. I am so proud to see students who were in my youth group still succeeding in my home town and other states, and even other countries today. Those were some fun and more carefree years.

One of the more creative ways I earned money during college was through car auctions. My lifelong mentor, Larry A., helped fuel my fire through our many hours of attending these car auctions. He would let me tag along while he went to check his gas and oil wells. Larry A. was a true father who gave without trying to take back. He loved and invested many hard hours coaching, challenging, and teaching me and telling me business, church ministry, family, and financial stories of all kinds. He would help me pick a car or truck, and then I would park them in the front yard of my house and put them up for sale. Luckily, my mom loved me more than she did not love having a used car lot in front of her house with two to four cars on it at all times. I'm so thankful she only nagged me about it, but never made me stop. Until the day I left to move to Virginia Beach to pursue my master's degree, I was selling my last car: a cherry red convertible. I didn't actually turn a good profit on that one, but it was fun to drive.

Leaving the hills of West Virginia, my creek, my friends, my church, and my new girlfriend, Jami, was a very difficult choice for me, as you can imagine. I delayed a couple of semesters, but finally got pushed out of my safe little nest, packed up a U-Haul, and moved to Virginia. When I moved to Virginia Beach, my first job was as a prayer counselor at CBN (Christian Broadcasting Network) across the campus from Regent University. That was quite a memorable and truly enjoyable experience for me.

During that same time, I had also started brokering seller-financed notes that my Uncle Gary turned me on to. While in Virginia, I continued to run ads in West Virginia and then in Kentucky and some other rural areas. People who were collecting monthly payments on homes and land they had sold would call me. I had large company buyers whom I had located through a training course my uncle let me borrow and who would buy these notes. If I could get the seller of the note to agree to $10,000, for example, and the big-end buyer said they would pay $12,000, I got to keep the $2,000 in the middle. That was a slow but steady business for me.

I was also a security guard at Founders Inn in Virginia Beach while I was doing my graduate work. I enjoyed that job more than any job in my life. I loved walking the beautiful grounds there and taking in the views of Swan Terrace with its immaculate landscaping and water views. There was never a more safe, simple job, and I was permitted to multitask during part of my nightshift. I got many of my master's degree papers written during those shifts. I also met some great coworkers, some of whom ended up selling houses with my team years later.

Around the same time, a friend from church named Bill got me turned on to a new idea. He was also a traveling idea salesperson like me. He showed me that finding land for builders could prove to be financially rewarding. That was my first real estate job in Hampton Roads. I was working hard every night after my doctoral work and my teaching responsibilities were done for the day. My day started around 9:30 a.m. and often went until two or three a.m. I would go from vacant lot to vacant lot, researching the owners of the land. Then, the next day, I would call the owners in the early evening and see if they would sell my builder their land.

My teaching responsibilities at that time included teaching and serving as an academic dean for Tidewater Bible College. That teaching and leadership opportunity opened the door to a couple of truly amazing professors, including Dr. J. Flynn and Dr. J. Umidi. They allowed me to co-teach, which led to teaching opportunities for Regent University. I taught modular courses in Washington, D.C., and evening and online courses at the Virginia Beach campus. My favorite topic was Life and Leadership Coaching. Coaching was the most significant coursework I did while at Regent. I was fortunate to become friends with and work for Dr. Umidi and Tony Stoltzfus at Regent in the leadership coaching office. That was such a developmental time, and I wouldn't trade those days for any money offered. I loved the school itself, as well as the study of church history, church growth, world evangelization, and one of my favorite topics: church planting. It is no coincidence that we are now applying those principles with our Fit Realty brokerage growth model.

So just how did I, a country boy-turned preacher, teacher, real estate agent, and team starter grow all of this success in the field of real estate? It has been, and continues to be, a journey, a daily struggle, and a battle for the achievement of dreams and worthwhile goals. I couldn't do it without being surrounded by trusted partners and a decisive staff. Our combined drive, hard work, dedication, and never-give-up attitude are the keys to our success!

CHAPTER 1

UNLESS THE MIND CAN CONCEIVE AND BELIEVE, IT CAN NEVER ACHIEVE:

WALKING YOUR DREAMS AND GOALS INTO REALITY

Towards the end of high school and the beginning of early college, my love for working out and building my muscles was a natural high and passion for me. On occasion, I would let myself dream of pursuing that secret heart goal. One day, after my first year of college, I was flexing in front of a mirror at the gym in my underwear when my friend, Dustin, walked in. Dustin was a bodybuilder. He asked me if I had ever considered getting into bodybuilding. He believed I had the physique to compete. I said yes, that was actually something I had always wanted to do. He told me he could teach me what to eat and what to do to get into the proper shape if I was interested. So, I did. I listened to everything he said, and I ultimately ended up competing in three or four bodybuilding competitions. I got up on stage in a tiny red bikini and flexed and posed in front of hundreds of strangers. Bodybuilding was never a long-term goal or lifestyle I wanted. It was just something I wanted to challenge myself to do, a thing I wanted to achieve and experience. I tried and tried to come up with ways to justify staying with the hard work of bodybuilding, but after asking all the questions I could come up with and attending some great events, I decided it was not something I wanted to invest in long-term. So, I dropped it and was thankful for the experience and my dear friends Dustin V. and John G. for being by my side in that adventure. All that to say, no matter the dream, no matter the goal, even if it is walking on stage in red underwear, if you want it, make it happen!

A dream is an unrefined hope, an aspiration, a what if, an imagined thing you might do or experience someday. Dreams are cost-free. You can think about them without making any commitment or taking any steps to do them. A dream is not a goal. Goals are specific future targets that we are committed to becoming or accomplishing in an action-oriented, time-specific way. One of the hardest parts of achieving dreams and goals is overcoming the mental barrier, realizing that you really can achieve this, and understanding that it's not as big as it appears.

Why should I dream beyond where I am? When we get caught up in the cares of the present, we sometimes find ourselves entangled with the day-to-day, unable to look beyond where we are. This is called existence. You may stay in one job that you don't like for twenty years, merely existing rather than dreaming of and achieving work that is much more satisfying. By dreaming, reflecting, and looking forward to where we ideally want to be, we can incrementally move toward a more significant and fulfilling life.

Does a dream have to be a big, long-term, world-changing type of dream? Absolutely not. Your dream may be to buy a house, launch a business, lose weight and feel better about yourself, start or expand a nonprofit ministry, contact a family member that you haven't spoken to for years, or get your life or schedule under control so that you can sleep better at night. You must first dream.

When you are working hard to fulfill a dream, keep a New Year's resolution, or achieve a goal, it's so easy to grow bored and weary. On the first of January, folks draft a list of resolutions that they believe they should keep: new things they want to learn, bad habits they want to unlearn, or things they want to create or build. The list is as unique as the individual. One of the most common resolutions is to get in shape or exercise daily. The gym fills up for a few weeks in January and then it empties just as quickly in February as folks lose their steam. They burn out, get frustrated, or figure out they just weren't that committed to making the time, working hard, and following through with a plan to make their resolution a reality.

It doesn't have to end like that. Don't give up before you even begin. When you start with a dream for which you have great interest and passion, it's easy to stay energetic and enthusiastic, particularly in the beginning. The difficulties often begin when you try to keep the momentum going and stay motivated for the long haul. Each one of us is capable of imagining—weaving creative thoughts in which we craft art, have a fabulous home or a lovely garden, come up with a successful work proposal, have a joyous family life, write an exceptional college term paper, or maybe even write a song. The creative process and its products is endless and unique to its creators. We all have opportunities to create things big and small if we courageously open ourselves to the process and are willing to explore dreams and abilities. If we're willing to follow our passion, if we're willing to try, to give it a shot or to let our hair down just a bit, each one of us is capable of doing great things.

Dream From the Heart

Your imagination is the place to begin. Imagination is the catalyst of possibility. Creativity is born into the DNA of every human walking this earth. The life you want to live can only be imagined by you and can only be created by you. No matter how sad, uninspired, or difficult your life is right now, you can imagine living a life with higher potentials and possibilities than the one you are living right now. Dare to play with your imagination. Dare to wonder what life could be like if you were in control of making it happen. You have the ability to paint a new life. You're the canvas, the paint, the paint brush, and the painter of your own life. Set aside some time to reconnect with your heart's dream. What have you put on the back burner that you can bring into your painting? What are the dreams you have for yourself? Not for your spouse, your family, or anyone else. What are YOUR dreams? If you don't like the way you feel in the life already painted, it's time to pick up the paint brush and paint a new life. You don't need to know exactly all the details of what your new life would look like. When you imagine a new life, you paint a doorway into a better life. Beyond that doorway, you begin to generate the potential of the life you want to live. Only you can imagine what that possibility would look like and how you would feel living that life. If you aren't certain, pretend. Make something up. You get to paint an entirely new life, and you get to do it poorly or wonderfully. If it turns out not looking and feeling quite as expected, you're still holding the paintbrush and the paint. You can adjust, modify, or paint over something not quite right.

Cultivate Belief

As you stand in front of the doorway you've painted, you probably won't have much belief that you can have the dream you imagined. Belief is something that develops over time. It grows as you continue to spend time at the doorway, looking at your dream, saying hello to it, and loving it, even while it's still just a possibility. Belief unfurls as you dare to take those first few steps through the doorway. Each day, as you acknowledge your dream, as you get excited about your dream, as you develop a committed relationship with your dream and as you decide you are worthy of having what you want, your belief deepens. It's okay to have fear as you step through the doorway. Fear often means you're headed in the right direction. The fear signals that this is something you want. Fear pops up because you don't yet know how to get what you want, and you don't want to risk failing. You don't want to be disappointed. Instead of letting fear stop you, choose to see it as a sign that you really do want to live your dream life. Unless the mind can conceive and believe, it can never achieve. Some of my greatest breakthroughs, both personally and in my entrepreneurial journey, were when I did it afraid. I walked headfirst into what I would now call seasons of tremendous chaos. Chaos is uncomfortable, and our human nature often triggers a fear response. You can freeze in fear, or you can do it afraid.

Have you ever heard of the flea experiment? You can place fleas in a jar with a lid on it. The fleas will, of course, begin to jump, repeatedly hitting the lid in their attempt to escape. After about 20 minutes, the fleas will realize they can't escape and will stop jumping so high to avoid smacking their head on the lid. Once they become accustomed to the fact that they can't escape, you can remove the lid, and the fleas will continue to jump at the same height, never escaping the jar. Since the fleas believe they can't escape the confines of the jar, they stop trying. Because of their experience with smacking their heads repeatedly every time they tried to escape, they never even bother looking up to see that the lid is no longer there.

Do not be afraid to look up every once in a while when working on your own dreams. What was once normal for you, what you once believed to be true, may change with time. You do not want to be like the fleas and remain stagnant in one place for fear of bumping your head again.

Dream Busters

As you are dreaming, pay attention to what's going on inside of you. Is there anything rising up inside saying: "I could never do this," or "I don't have enough education," or "This couldn't happen to me," or "I'm sure I would just blow it if I had the opportunity." Notice the strong feelings rising up inside: Failure. Rejection. Looking stupid. Sounding dumb. Seeming flaky. Seeming materialistic. These fears are dream busters. Dream busters are rooted in:

- **Childhood Tapes**—"You'll never amount to anything," or "That's not practical. Do you think money grows on trees?" or "You're a good starter, but a terrible finisher," or "You're just not that smart," or "You're so lazy," or "You will never be able to maintain a long-term healthy relationship."
- **Self-Defeating Beliefs**—These stop you before you even get started. "I'm not good in math," or "If something is fun, it can't be good to spend time doing it," or "Other people succeed in life, but I never will," or "I don't have anything to say or do that people will really pay for."
- **Past Failures and Hurts**—"I tried that once and I got burned," or "I keep thinking about how we lost our house when dad tried to start a business," or "I failed in school last time," or "The last time I tried a vacation it was a disaster," or "My last marriage was a mess. I'll just blow it again."

All of the above is common. Most of us are secretly and subconsciously afraid to dream. To genuinely dream, you have to throw off your limitations. You have to believe that you have unlimited resources. You have to believe that you will succeed.

You can't be logical. What have you always wanted to do in your life? What do you dream of accomplishing or being? Push out beyond what seems comfortable. It's okay to dream fun dreams. These are your dreams, and you can change them as you become clear on what you want, but you have to start somewhere!

Create a Vision of Success

Great achievers have a habit. They see themselves living the life of their dreams. They imagine already having what they want. Teach yourself to visualize yourself succeeding. See the light at the end of the tunnel before even starting. Create an inner dialog of success and allow yourself to already feel the feelings of achievement.

Imagine the difference between these two scenarios: The first person, Gail, walks around with a clear vision of herself having already achieved her goals. Multiple times each week, month, and year she pulls up her dream and spends time with the physical excitement of imagining a successful outcome. Every day she speaks life-giving words to herself and leads herself with strength, kindness, and compassion. She plays with her dream, offering it a relationship of love. When obstacles occur, she may fall flat, but at some point she remembers her vision. She fans the flames, the fire in her belly reignites, and her energy returns to chase her dreams.

A second person, Ben, has not yet developed the ability to hold tightly to a vision. The first obstacle comes along and knocks him flat on the ground. Ben stays there, accepting his defeat. His dream is buried as he decides the failure is proof he can't have what he wants. His inner dialog is self-critical. He feels frustration, anger, discouragement, disgust, and the hopelessness of "what's the point?"

Both Gail and Ben are going to run into obstacles. Both will meet with disappointment, fear, and failure. There is no avoiding them. However, who is more likely to achieve their dreams: Gail or Ben?

My mentor, Larry A., would often challenge my "stinking thinking," and he would assign me projects regularly. One of those assignments was to write down a page full of positive things about my life, overall things that were true, whether deep or very simple. After a few weeks, I was shocked at the level of change my brain and then my emotions went through and how my thinking had begun to transform. I realized I was a generally pessimistic person. I was very hard on myself, second guessing all of my decisions. Over a period of time, with quite a bit of effort to wash my brain with truth, it actually happened: My stinking thinking had begun to be a thing of the past. It creeps up every now and then, but I fight it off with a few good habits.

Let Yourself Shift for Higher Value

There is no way that dreams can ever become reality if we aren't willing to let go of what is of lesser value in our current lives. It doesn't mean that we don't still appreciate those things and that we didn't grow from having them in our lives. It just means that sometimes, in order to make space for higher value in our lives, there are activities and people that must be let go.

We are all born dreamers, but as we become adults and we inevitably meet life's hardships, our self-confidence and our ability to achieve can be altered. As we grow older, some of us no longer dare to dream for fear of appearing childish or being disappointed. You can give into your natural broken human nature and just disregard, discredit, and devalue your dreams, or you can choose to build the strong habits that will allow you to achieve your dreams and push you to take calculated risks to achieve more.

In addition, we as human beings are conditioned to survive in a threatening environment when resources are scarce, and we're genetically structured to be alert to real and imagined dangers everywhere. Life, from this perspective, is a hostile culture where everyone is competing with one another in the struggle to have enough and be enough. Although this is true and we must compete with all we have, we also need to approach our lives with a view of abundance, a belief that there is more than enough business, wealth, and friendship available. In the United States and other capitalist countries, competition is the vehicle to success, and the triumphs of some imply the failure of others. I cannot really argue that reality. For example, Amazon arrives on the scene, and competing smaller companies across the country go into bankruptcy. Our environment is perceived as a pie that has a limited number of slices. From this viewpoint, life is truly limited from all aspects. Whether it is trying to locate that right spouse or that perfect rental property, don't let your eyes be blinded with a negative, "there is not enough" viewpoint.

You must think of life compared to a pie differently. In the realm of all possibilities, the pie is whole, and each time we take a slice, it becomes whole again. When we live from this perspective, we no longer need to compare ourselves with others. Accordingly, vision-led dreams spring out from a perspective of abundance. I have evolved as a tremendously competitive person, much more so than in my younger years. Many people have taken from my companies, attacked my companies, or tried to take my key staff and my key agents. Competitors have copied me each step of the way. At the end of the day, however, there is enough for all of us who are willing to work hard. You want to copy my idea? Oh well, there are a million more ideas I can implement. The one you stole was getting old anyway! Compete? Yes! Fight to win? Yes! Battle for your piece of the pie with all you have; however, when those days come when someone eats the pie you had planned to eat, do not let it drain your energy. Accept that they got the better of you; good job for them. There's another big piece waiting on you. Forget what is behind you and focus on the possibilities in front of you!

Practically speaking, when you have a business and you imagine there's an abundance of consumers out there who need your services, you're more likely to take action and find ways to reach these consumers than if you entertain the thought that consumers and resources are scarce and limited. I've watched this type of self-defeating attitude keep many business men and women from taking their business past a survival level. Your clients need you as badly as you need them. Your gifts are needed. Your products are needed, whether they're your own talents or the copy machine or the car you sell. Someone needs what you have. What you're longing for, needing, or missing is longing for, needing and missing *you*. When our vision is oriented towards abundance and possibilities, we may more easily concede a short-term goal in pursuit of a bigger dream. When confronted to a limiting belief about a situation, here are a few questions you can ask yourself: Is it true? How do I know this is always true? How can I think about this in a way that will allow me to move forward?

Make a Decision

Do you know the fable of the eagle and the chicken? When the eagle was very small, he fell from the safety of his nest. A chicken farmer found the eagle, brought him to the farm, and raised him in a chicken coop among his many chickens. The eagle grew up believing he was a chicken and doing what chickens do: eating from the ground and pecking the worms like those who surrounded him. Inside, the eagle had a dream. He had a vision. He could see the sky and wanted to feel the clouds in his wings. Are you still pecking at worms when you could be soaring and eating fresh meat? Choose to embrace what is inside and fly above the comfortable!

Once you have a dream, decide that you want to live this kind of happy and gratified life. This may seem basic, but many people never decide and commit fully to their dream—they just keep thinking about it. Or, when the first (or second, third, fourth, or fifth) obstacle appears, they give up. Make a commitment to yourself. Now is not the time to worry about how to make it happen. Instead, plant the seed of your dream inside of you and commit to loving this seed until the day you can harvest the fruits of your efforts. You must decide in advance that each time you get knocked down, you won't let it linger. Cry. Pound the pillow. Use some fancy profanities. Then, suck it up buttercup!

Get creative. Get your whiteboard out. Lay out all your options to overcome the obstacles and get started more confidently than ever. Not weeks later or months later, but hours later. Your life, your choice. Nobody will care more about you than you, so the quicker you can accept that, the better, my friend. Honor your commitment to self. No one can let you down more than you can. Make a commitment about what you want and stand strong in your commitment. No matter how challenging, how fearful, or how overwhelming it may seem, decide you are going for it! Why? For no other reason than because you want it. This is something you want for yourself and a choice you have made.

Decide where you are now and what seems like the right place to begin. Action means starting at the right place at the right time. Action steps may mean first spending time imagining what is wanted and what a joyful life would look like. Action steps may require writing down your dream, putting your dream into picture form, spending time each day visualizing and feeling your dream, or taking the steps to break down an overwhelming change into smaller, manageable steps. It might take weeks or even months of doing these steps before you're ready to move on to the next level of action. There's no step too small. Take the step that feels right for right now, and you're already living your dream.

Relationship Flow

Imagine you have a bucket of live crabs. In this bucket, some of the crabs could easily escape, but other crabs pull them back down to prevent any from getting out, thus ensuring the group's collective demise. The crab bucket mentality: "If I can't have it, neither can you." The analogy to human behavior is that members of a group will attempt to reduce the self-confidence of any member who achieves success beyond the others out of envy, spite, conspiracy, or competitive feelings to halt their progress.

While you don't want to be surrounded by negative people in your life, relationships are an important aspect of our dreams. A lot of people suffer in their younger age because of their need to be independent and their expectation for everything in life to be perfect. Once you discover the power of being interdependent, you can enjoy the beauty of healthy and balanced relationships. These are relationships that allow you to give without fear of never receiving. Helping other people make their dreams a reality is an interdependent way to live. The people you allow to regularly speak into your life will shape the way you think, whether for the good or for the bad. Be aware of that. Intentionally spend time with people who believe in you and inspire you.

Another important lesson Larry A. taught me was to be a thermostat, not a thermometer. Thermostats are set by the owner and they tell the home system what temperature to stick to. Thermometers, on the other hand, simply read the temperature in the room and adapt to the environment. While on your entrepreneurial journey, sometimes even your closest friends and family who love you the most will question your actions. If you're surrounded by negativity, you must choose to be your own thermostat and work to get the temperature back to the degree that *you* set.

Feed Yourself

Living in the space between dreams and reality requires a lot of energy. Feed yourself knowledge for your mind, feed yourself real food from the earth for your body, and feed your soul by finding something creative to do that makes time disappear. One of the biggest reasons people don't dream is they simply don't take care of themselves to have the energy to do so. If you're frazzled, stressed, and emotionally drained, how can you feed yourself? Tired eyes never see a bright future! It's vitally important that you keep your mind on things that are good and uplifting and bring you life even in the hardest times of the journey. Mature people do not need others to constantly pump them up like a tire going flat. Mature people can pump their own tires. They can push themselves to get up and take that next action step, even when they don't feel like it. There are times, typically every few years, when I'm hit so hard in business by people, circumstances, market conditions, or new federal laws that I literally turn off all devices and lie in the dark, pray, cry, cuss, run, read, journal, or basically do whatever I need to do to work through it. After I lick my wounds, I start to give myself some pep talks. I look in the mirror and remind myself that I'm a guy who will not give up, no matter what or who comes against my business efforts. You should do that too. Look in the mirror and remind yourself when you must. Remind yourself that you are your best investment; you are the only YOU on this earth; your life has meaning, impact and influence; and yes, you do matter.

Start Applying These Principles

Start spending some time every day focusing on your life vision. You don't have to know what it is at this point. Just commit to spending a minimum of ten minutes each day with the following question: "What do I want to experience in my life now while I'm eager and vibrant?" As you ask yourself this question, it's important to realize the timeliness of it. You are asking yourself what you want to experience *not* in a near or far or uncertain future, but in this very moment. Contemplate what you really want to experience during this precious time you've been blessed with on Earth. If you think you don't have ten minutes a day for this, recognize this as a limiting thought and move yourself beyond it. Make this time, ten minutes each day, consistently for one month. Start a journal, write the question, and let your inner voice come through. Can you give yourself that gift?

In the beginning, when you start asking this question, you'll find that your mind can't easily see beyond what it believes is possible for you. It's important that you allow it to expand beyond these limits. Even when you find it difficult to believe, plow forward and write down everything that comes to your mind without censoring or limiting what arises. Let your imagination soar. If your mind argues that it is unrealistic and senseless, let it argue. Eventually you'll find that your thoughts loosen up and begin to tap into new realms of possibilities. Brainstorm with your life coach, with a mentor, or with someone who can ask the right questions and help you unpack your options. Your intuitive self will start shooting through. All you need to do is trust the process and show up every day consistently. After you've finished writing each day, read over it. Does anything strike you? Underline any passages or phrases that stand out. If you're more of a visual person, you could start collecting stacks of magazines and cut out any pictures that appeal to you without thinking about why or analyzing them. When you have a pile of pictures, look for both fresh ideas and common themes. Paste them into a scrapbook and add to them as you come across other images that appeal to you.

If you stick to these exercises for some time, you'll start to identify patterns and ideas that will give you clues regarding your life vision or big dream. There's no right way to do these exercises, and the only way to do them wrong is to fail to be persistent with them. If you find that some days nothing happens or comes out, let it be okay. Just make sure it doesn't prevent you from being there for yourself the next day. Consistency is key to anything you wish to realize in life. Another benefit from these exercises is that as you start focusing on your dreams, you'll gradually shift your mindset from what separates you from them to what you can do today to move towards them. The distinction between these two apparently opposite ways of apprehending life may appear radically twofold and even simplistic. However, rather than stating that one approach is wrong and the other is right, the idea here is to see how we can be empowered by allowing ourselves to dream and expand our range of possibilities.

Once you've chosen the dream that feels right for you, make a list of the resources and the necessary steps to realize it. Setting clear action steps and then tracking those action steps is an essential activity to maximize each week, month, and year of your life. Take a half of a day every three months and review your progress. Keep it written or typed and easy to find. Keep your goals near you. Hang them on the wall if that's what works best for you. Truly successful people don't allow their dreams and driving motivators to be forgotten. It's a daily, a weekly, a life habit and muscle that we all must build.

Now, ask yourself what would be a first step to start moving towards realization. What would be a second step? And another? What would it take for you to start today, moving in the direction of your dream? Would it be worth it? What is the biggest potential that can unfold in the pursuit of your dream? When you say yes to one thing, you're saying no to something else. Many times, we don't take the time to think, "If I say yes to this, what am I saying no to without even realizing it?" Your time is limited. Giving five hours each week to one thing means you don't have five hours to give to something else.

Visualize Your Dream Home

Think of real estate as an example of achieving a tangible life dream. There's a reason many people say part of the American dream is home ownership. Land and homes are the foundation of wealth, security, and safety. You build wealth as you pay down your home mortgage rather than when you pay rent. You also typically grow wealth as a result of inflation and property values increasing. Home ownership is a dream worth chasing.

You'll need paper, a pen or pencil and, initially, an hour or so of uninterrupted time; however, this is an ongoing exercise and something you can keep adding to until you're completely satisfied with the end result. Start by writing, "My Dream

Home" in the center of the page and drawing a circle or a heart around it, whatever takes your fancy. Next, sketch in lines leading out from the center, like a starburst, and write down all the things you want in your dream home. You can start by writing down basics like electricity, gas supply, main sewage, and telephone line, or you can assume those are going to be there anyway. Are you going to purchase a re-sale home or are you going to explore options to build a new home? Do you like sleek and modern or something more traditional? Is it important that your home is well insulated, has central heating, and/or double-glazed windows? Write that down. You're going to have to answer an awful lot of questions to get clear about what you want, but it's going to be worth it. You cannot get what you want until you know what you want.

How many stories do you want? Would you want a one-story ranch because stairs are painful for your knees or maybe because you have an aging parent living with you? How many bedrooms do you want, and why do you want that number? If you want one as an office or a work room, could you just as easily have a dining room that doubles up? Do you want a wet bar in your master bedroom and a huge double shower so you can stretch and steam each morning? Is this home going to last you forever or are you creating something for now, knowing that as your needs change you will be able to create another dream home?

This is your dream you're creating here, and you make up the rules as you go along. If you find yourself thinking, "I'll never be able to afford that!" etcetera, tear down your walls of limited belief. Doing this exercise not only helps you gain clarity about what you like and what you want, it also helps you get in touch with those limiting beliefs that stop you from being who you really are and getting what you really want. The more work you do on this, the greater your chances of success because you are also working on your subconscious. You're giving your subconscious encouraging affirmations and wiping clear the old negative tapes and replacing them with new, positive ones.

If you go through this exercise and realize that you dreamed of your second or third home, but right now you need to start with a small townhouse to get your first home under your belt, that's normal and expected. Don't be discouraged. Be encouraged! You need to know where you want to end up to be sure you take the best steps to eventually get there. Enjoy the now, but keep your eyes on the prize. Sacrifice a little now to get more of what you want later. Getting what you want but what you can't quite afford can become a burden rather than a blessing. It's better to live in a smaller home and be at peace with your finances than it is to live in a larger, more expensive home and worry constantly about making your payments.

When you get to the point where you have had enough, stop. You're doing some really hard work here, and you need to acknowledge that. We are generally much better at quantifying physical work than mental effort, and it's important not to overdo things at this stage. Otherwise, you will end up exhausted, especially at the beginning. Put it to one side and come back to it later, but try and set aside a brief time each day, or perhaps three times a week, to keep working on your blueprint.

As your vision grows, start imagining yourself in your dream home, walking around it, looking at each room. How do you feel? Are you comfortable? Does it reflect who you are and who you would like to be? What colors dominate? Lush, rich colors or something more subtle? Are there carpets, wood floors, rugs, or runners? Is it full of things? Is it a cozy family home, or is it elegant and minimalist? What do the doors look like? The walls? The lights? If you change your mind about something as your vision develops, that's fine. Just change it on your blueprint. It doesn'tt matter how messy it gets. You can always do a neater version as you get more clarity.

Something that should emerge while doing this exercise is a sense of responsibility for what you are creating, and that can be tricky. On one hand, go for whatever you want. On the other hand, you have to take responsibility for what you create. It doesn't smake sense to want a large garden with a vegetable patch if no one in the family has ever picked up a shovel, or to want an elegant, minimalist home you saw in a classy magazine when you know you're really untidy and perfectly happy with that. You need to be realistic. This dream home has to be in line with your values and what you want out of life.

The most important consequence of doing this exercise is gaining clarity about who you are and what you want. We so often spend our lives vaguely dissatisfied, not sure what we want, but quite sure that we don't want what we have. Ultimately, you may end up taking a few tiny steps to bring your dream into reality, clearing out stuff you no longer need or changing the use of a room from a bedroom into a work room or office. Or, you might move in huge leaps and acquire exactly what you wished for! You may decide you aren't quite ready for such major change and that there are other issues to resolve first.

That's also fine. You might want to put your blueprint away for a while and come back to it in six months or a year. It just might astonish you to look at it after that time and see that some of the things you wrote down have appeared, as though by magic. Once you get really clear about what you want, what you want tends to find you!

Keep working on your blueprint until you're confident you've covered every possible detail. Then, start putting energy into moving towards that dream. What will move you closer? What do you need to let go of?

Enjoy the Process!

Each person has within them individual ideas of what's exciting, whether it be their dream house or something else completely different. This exciting idea comes from deep within, from the center. It has no logical basis. It's an idea of creation. Remember, no one is making you do this. This is your dream for yourself. Some people may support you; others may not. Remember, it's not their dream and not their obligation to make it happen for you. Your responsibility to yourself and to your life is to imagine your dream, to grow belief in your dream, and to summon excitement during the process of making your dream a reality. Creating your dream will require emotional, spiritual, and physical effort. Fall in love with the journey itself, not just the outcome. When you achieve a portion of your goal or a major action step, take a few hours and pat yourself on the back. Celebrate your successful achievement of a worthwhile goal. Then, get back to work! If you sacrificed financially for months and now have a pay day, a closed transaction or a big bonus, go ahead and spend a little on yourself or your family and reward that effort! That small reward will help you stay in it for the long game.

Turn Your Dream into a Goal

Now comes the fun: taking this realm of ideas and brainstorming and laying the foundation for the achievement of the goal. All worthwhile goals require sacrifice and work, but by continually achieving worthwhile goals, you'll find success in the areas you choose to focus. The point of this is not to make the right plan, but to get specific enough with what you can see now to count the cost. Unless you're willing to start with an imperfect plan, you'll probably never start at all.

S.M.A.R.T. Goal

Specific: A goal is specific when you can describe it in a concrete way.

Example: "I want to start a business," is not a specific goal. Instead, "I want to start an interior design business that produces $45,000 per year by the time I'm 35."

Measurable: You need to be able to tell when you've accomplished this goal.

Example: "I want to be a better father," is not specific enough. How will you know when you've achieved it? Instead, "I want to improve my fathering skills by reading one book on parenting every two months and meeting with a more experienced father one time per month."

Attainable: It can't be a lofty dream that isn't realizable.
Example: "I want to make $100,000 this year as a real estate agent." If it's April and the class you need to take to become a real estate agent starts in May and is three months long, you may not be able to attain this goal in the five remaining months of the year.

Relevant: A goal is relevant when it's important to you and when it references your values.
Example: "I want to get a new job over the next nine months so that when my wife has her baby she can be a full-time mom, as she has always wanted."

Time Specific: Goals are not opened-ended. They have dates attached.
Example: "I want to start a homeless shelter." This is not time-specific. Instead, "In the next twelve months I want to get the necessary training needed to open a homeless shelter within the next five years."

Estimating Time:

Let's practice estimating how much time each part of your goal will take. This way, you'll learn to accurately measure your time. If you continually underestimate it, you'll grow disappointed and have to struggle harder not to give up.

- Use small steps. If you break your goal into big chunks, it's likely your estimate will be way off.

- Establish benchmarks from previous experience. Or, as you get going, pay attention to how long something takes so you can make your goal even more precise.
- Consider friction. A fifteen-minute phone call may take thirty minutes because of phone tag. Keep this type of thing in mind as you set your action steps.
- Do not massage the numbers when you add up the time it'll take to accomplish your goal. If it seems like it'll take longer than you first thought, give yourself permission to alter the timeline so your goals remain realistic and achievable. Sometimes things take longer than they initially appear, but don't get discouraged. Important goals take time!
- Get feedback! Any time you lay out an estimate, let two or three pairs of eyes take a look at it, especially your spouse or a trusted mentor. We can subconsciously adjust the numbers to fit our time or resources. Personality will play a big role in whether you're overly optimistic in what you can accomplish in a certain amount of time or pessimistic in terms of overestimating how long something will take.

Make Your S.M.A.R.T. Goal Even Smarter

Put your goal out there and let your coach, mentor, and trusted friends help you smarten it up! Make notes on the insights you glean as you talk and brainstorm. Examples: "Sharpen that a little. Can you be more specific?" or "Do you have a clear enough picture to estimate what it will take in terms of time, money, and energy to reach this goal?" or "How will you know when you've accomplished that goal? Could you make it more measurable?" or "Could you clarify how much time this will take for you to accomplish?"

Turning Your Goal into Action Steps

If you're serious about seeing your dreams become a reality, you must get serious about putting your action steps into your calendar. Write down individual steps that can be scheduled. If you add three hours to your weekly calendar, you'll need to cut three hours of something else out. Don't say, "I really don't need to write these steps down; I'll remember them in my head." It's only when we begin taking action steps and making schedule changes that we move in earnest toward our goals.

WORKSHEET:
TURNING YOUR S.M.A.R.T. GOAL INTO ACTION STEPS

Brainstorm here:

_____

_____

_____

_____

_____

_____

My one action step for the next seven days:

_____

_____

_____

_____

_____

_____

The person I will ask to hold me accountable to this step:

_____

_____

_____

_____

_____

CHAPTER 2

CONNECTING TO YOUR GIVE-A-DAMN:
BECOMING AN ENTREPRENEUR

I was never a very good student academically growing up. I struggled with my colors, then with my math, then my English. The list goes on. My parents were happy if I was able to make a "C" average. There was a point, however, after my first year of college, when I woke up and realized that I had to care. Once I connected my "give-a-damn" to what mattered and what was valued long-term, I started making A's and B's. It turned out I simply wasn't owning control over my own mind, body, and the direction of my life. I realized that nobody, no parent, no friend, and no mentor was going to succeed in my life for me. They could help on occasion, but ultimately, day after day, my life was my decision. That change in mindset helped me obtain my undergraduate degree with a double major in marketing and business management with a minor in psychology. After that, I went on to Regent University and obtained a double master's degree in church history and church doctrine with a specialty in leadership coaching. Then, I was given several opportunities to teach masters and doctorate courses in Washington, D.C., and Virginia Beach. I was also an academic dean for a season at a small bible college in Virginia Beach. I loved teaching and still consider it one of my passions. However, I knew that if I ever wanted to make a sufficient living as a teacher, I would need to further my education. One of my proudest accomplishments is obtaining my doctorate from Regent University. It wasn't easy for me. I don't have a photographic memory to help me study. I had to work at and study academics much harder than many people I knew. Not only did I have to work harder academically, but I also worked several small entrepreneurial businesses while going through school. One of my professors allowed me to start a company as a class project. It was the International Coaching Network. I had a website built, and I set up pay-per-click advertising and sold life-coaching packets. I also made some money running small ads in newspapers across rural states by brokering seller financed mortgage notes. This helped me fall in love with real estate for the first time. Setting my own pay was a new experience for me. Ultimately, it was tough to manage business and focus on school, but I never gave up. I pushed through and achieved that goal of obtaining my doctorate.

Why Be an Entrepreneur

The biggest reward of becoming an entrepreneur is the personal satisfaction that comes from having the freedom to make your own business decisions and then act on them. It's also a great feeling to provide jobs, opportunities and advancement to more and more employees and independent contractors as you grow a great company. Influence is the ability to change the course of someone's future. Business ownership is a type of influence. You need to steward your influence. Let it grow, and let it impact the lives of others. That is one rewarding part of entrepreneurship. You cannot impact the lives of others without influence. You can meet someone, see talent, take action, hire them, and train them, and at the same time you made a true impact by helping someone provide for their families and further their careers and life dreams, all inside the business you started. When you own a business, you get to be your own boss. There is value in the fact that no person can fire you. They can all leave you high and dry, but they can't fire you. You can get new people if you have a good business system. There is no limit to what an entrepreneur can financially create. My father always told me, "Healthy things grow." Maintain your buildings, equipment, and businesses well. Expect your business to grow and take action to inspire that growth in an ongoing way.

Advantages and Disadvantages of Entrepreneurship

The entrepreneur gets the chance to participate in a venture they enjoy. This increases the chances of success in the venture, since the individual is passionate and dedicated to work for the venture. Entrepreneurship offers flexibility to the entrepreneur, allowing them to participate in family and social activities. An entrepreneur has the capacity to set a salary they believe is commensurate to their input, and this helps improve the level of motivation to achieve more.

On the other hand, entrepreneurship offers no guarantees of a regular paycheck, especially when the business is at its formative stage. Schedules are highly unpredictable, and the entrepreneur will be required to respond to changes in the market or customer requests almost immediately. This may, at times, require longer hours. As a serial entrepreneur, I cannot possibly count the jobs and roles I've filled over the years that I didn't enjoy at all. As the owner, I have had to step into the dirtiest parts of the job many times.

There are seasons of the entrepreneurial journey when you'll find joy in providing employment opportunities to others. There will also be times you'll be frustrated with your employees because humans make mistakes and employees may not be as driven as you would hope (or they may not put in those extra hours and energy that you as an entrepreneur will). Employees will not care as much as you, no matter how much you want them to. They will not feel your financial losses the way you feel them. Healthy expectations of your employees and customers/ clients is paramount in the mind game of growing a business. You have to be able to accept that sometimes you will be the last person to get paid, the last person to leave the office, and the *only* person who wakes up on a weekend and says, "I think I'll throw in an extra ten hours today."

Risks of Being an Entrepreneur

Being fully responsible means the success or failure of your business rests on you, the people you choose to employ, and how well you manage their efforts and performance. Unforeseeable problems will arise. Many new businesses don't make much money in the beginning, so you may not always be able to pay yourself. It's not unusual for entrepreneurs to work a significant amount of extra hours to make their businesses successful. This is especially true during the initial start-up process.

In your entrepreneurial adventures, please remember that you'll occasionally deserve to be fired from roles that you've filled as you flex and make things happen. Your staff will look at you, and you'll look at yourself, and you'll have to own mistakes or wrong directional decisions you've made. Be authentic with your staff when necessary. Own your error, and then forgive yourself and move the heck on! Never allow yourself to wallow in your anger or self-deprecation, even when you've fallen short or made a poor decision. That benefits no one. Just shake it off and rise up out of the ashes quickly.

Who Are Entrepreneurs?

Webster's Dictionary defines an entrepreneur as "One who organizes, manages, and assumes the risks of a business or enterprise." Yet, what this definition lacks is the significant distinction between an entrepreneur and a successful entrepreneur. Becoming a successful entrepreneur is the true goal. Who are the people who fit this pattern, and how are the successful ones different from the less successful? A successful entrepreneur is a unique businessperson who is ready to take a financial risk to attain the upside reward. They might be inventors, resellers of products, or people that offer their time, services and expertise in exchange for money, but the common thread is the desire and drive to succeed. Successful entrepreneurs are ready to do whatever it takes and wish to learn from those who've effectively demonstrated how to achieve their dream. It can be a different product or solution to a problem, but the basics are always the same.

Commonalities Among Successful Entrepreneurs

Self-assessment, or evaluating your strengths and weaknesses, is an important part of becoming an entrepreneur. Do you have what it takes to be a successful entrepreneur? Below are some characteristics and skills that many entrepreneurs have. You may not need all of them to be successful, but obviously the more you possess, the better. Try to make an honest self-assessment. Which characteristics and skills do you already possess, and which ones would you like to further grow or develop?

Personal Characteristics
- Courage
- Creativity
- Curiosity
- Determination
- Discipline
- Empathy
- Enthusiasm
- Flexibility

- Honesty
- Patience
- Responsibility

Skills

- Business skills
- Communication skills
- Computer skills
- Being a gifted speaker
- Decision-making skills
- Problem-solving skills
- Mathematical skills
- Organizational skills
- People skills
- Being a natural visionary

An attitude is a way of viewing or thinking about something that affects how you feel about it. Entrepreneurs tend to be people with positive attitudes. An aptitude is a natural ability to do a particular type of work or activity well.

Key Aptitudes:

- **Perseverance:** Business owners are usually determined to get past obstacles and see a project through its completion despite setbacks. They will overcome their frustrations and problems and persevere. Given the challenges of today's complex business environment, this aptitude is at the top of the list.

- **Self-Assurance:** Entrepreneurs show self-confidence and trust their instincts. This self-assurance helps them through difficult times and pushes them to achieve tough goals. Without that self-assurance, people hesitate and are not so willing to take calculated risks.
- **Creativity:** The aptitude of creativity comes in handy when entrepreneurs need to identify business opportunities. Entrepreneurs instinctively see gaps in the market and can find unique products and services that meet a demand.
- **Tolerance for Ambiguity:** Entrepreneurs are comfortable with ambiguity and are capable of making decisions even when they don't have all the information they need. For example, you might be selling products or services in a relatively unknown market. This level of uncertainty can be very stressful for most people, but entrepreneurs learn how to work around it.
- **Attitude Toward Failure:** Many business owners have a long history of failures and accept these as part of the learning process. Rather than view failure as a catastrophe, an entrepreneur will learn what to avoid the next time around. They will pick themselves up after a failure and start over. A motto I say over and over again is "fail forward every time." What did I learn from the failure? Write it down, reflect on the lesson, and enjoy the character development. Cry if you must. Kick, cuss, and stomp, but fail forward. Learn from each failure and then call it education. My dad joked me a hundred times in my early business years. He was always surprised at

the crazy business pickles I got myself into. He would say, "Well, you only lost $10,000. That was cheaper than a semester at school. You should write a thank-you letter to that guy for teaching you so much for just the $10,000 loss."

- **Action-Oriented:** Entrepreneurs must stay on their toes, be in position, and be ready for anything. The bigger your business grows, the more wild and crazy the issues. As an entrepreneur, you must be action-oriented each and every day - even if your neighbor's dog kept you awake half the night. Get in the shower, get yourself to work, and keep doing the work of growing your business. Don't put off difficult tasks until later. You must have a strong desire to tackle objectives.

- **Flexible:** Blessed are the flexible, for they shall not be broken! A willingness to be flexible can't be understated. There are times to be as stubborn as an old mule, but there are many more times that an entrepreneur must remain flexible.

Action Plan to be an Entrepreneur

Preparing yourself to start a business may seem like a formidable task. You may think you must learn specific skills, such as finance and business practices or how to manufacture and market products. Of course these topics are important, but they aren't difficult. If you just take an interest in them and start paying attention, you can learn about these subjects over time. You can also hire professionals to help you when you start a company. However, what makes the real difference is your strategy and your approach to business, which are reflections of your personal philosophy. Business is about transactions and dealing with people. Most business is based on a relationship built on a foundation of mutual trust. Below is a suggested plan of action to get you started.

- **Increase Your Potential:** Increase your business knowledge. Read magazines and newspaper articles, search the internet, and talk to business owners. Locate business mentors and spiritual fathers and mothers who will speak life into you during the high times and the low times of your journey. Strengthen your math skills. If you can't figure out if you're making money or losing money, you better keep practicing with a calculator and amortization charts or hire a bookkeeper—fast. Evaluate your strengths and weaknesses, and explore careers that interest you. Look for volunteering opportunities in different fields to expand your perspectives and find out if any companies in your area provide internship programs. Obtaining a good education benefits you personally and opens doors to more career opportunities. If you pick up one business concept each week, you'll learn a lot over time. You will learn how business works and how the business community looks at things. What is important is an attitude of active learning. Take an interest. Talk to people. Ask why things happen and how things work. Look at issues at your current job from a broader point of view. For example, when someone asks you to solve a technical problem, ask about the business context. Find out how the company decided the problem was worth solving. By doing so, you'll not only gain insights into business, but you'll also learn things that enable you to create a better technical solution and build problem-solving skills.

- **Develop a Strategy:** A good strategist is creative; they'll put together what they know to solve a problem. The keys to creativity are your knowledge base and your problem-solving skills. People who've been in business for a while tend to have street smarts with unusual ways of seeing things and solving problems. Business problems are different from technical problems in that they have more boundary conditions, and those boundary conditions are often poorly defined, unpredictable, and changing. So you also have to be extremely sensitive to your environment and constantly modifying your strategy as new information becomes available. Strategies must change as business environment, competitors, and technology change. Many times, strategy needs to be written in pencil with the willingness to adjust the plan yearly. Your scheduled planning cycles will help a lot. In physical sciences, we deal with well-defined principles and concrete answers. In business, we live with uncertainty. Like a chess player, you have to optimize complex situations and anticipate several moves in advance. The key to making better decisions is to hone your skills at comparing the likely outcomes of several scenarios. You can improve these skills if you develop a habit of reminding yourself to think ahead one more step. Constantly challenge yourself and think through problems. Is there a different way to interpret what that person said? What does he/she really want? Can I find a different way to satisfy that requirement? By thinking through every issue, you sharpen your problem-solving skills. Eventually you develop the ability to get to the heart of the matter pretty quickly, even when a new situation arises. The converse is also true: your problem-solving skills will atrophy if you become intellectually lazy.

- **Study the Environment:** You need to develop a sensitivity to business trends. You'll learn to correlate apparently unrelated events that affect what you do and incorporate them into your strategy. For example, if you intend to buy a property or your first home, you'll want to know the price of the building and compare it to your budget, as well as the location of the property and every other necessary thing about the property. Given that information, you might go ahead with the project, price your property aggressively in anticipation of further cost reductions, and decide to sell direct without any middleman. A sense of the environment can help you fine-tune your strategy.

- **Sell Yourself:** An entrepreneur is at times the person who pours gasoline on himself so that others come around to watch him burn. When you start a business and only get paid when sales or transactions happen, you must sell yourself. Get a logo on your hat, shirt, or car. Have pens to pass out and forget to take home from banks. Talk about your business while buying your new tires and at the grocery store while you pick out the weekend steaks. If you don't promote you, who's going to? If you don't spread the word, who do you think will? You are the entrepreneur. Embrace that reality and evangelize your brand.

- **Build a Strong Banking Relationship:** Regardless of the type of business you start, you can be assured that a good banker will bring you value and vice versa. A win-win banking relationship will ensure you have the resources to grow your business and to purchase whatever is necessary for your business. It's my opinion that you need at least two to three banking relationships at all times. In addition, you need two to four quality credit cards with high balances for special uses. You need to stay in tune with new products and finance options to grow your business. For example, I have had a $100,000 unsecured line of credit with a bank for twelve plus years. I cannot begin to explain how much peace of mind that line of credit has given me or how much money it has made for me over the past twelve years. Lending money to my own companies has almost always worked out very well for me, as my staff and my partners are good investments.

- **Build a Strong Relationship with a Trusted Attorney:** Once you are financially able to start an ongoing relationship with an attorney, don't delay. If after three years all of your employees leave you and go start their own business together, you're going to sorely regret that you didn't make the investment up front to protect your infant company. Your business is like your child. You need to protect it. My attorney, Barry D., is one of my dearest, most trusted advisors. The years that I was in business without a truly trusted attorney never felt quite right. I felt exposed and unnecessarily vulnerable, and I lost sleep for no good reason. In addition to a trusted attorney, get the proper insurance. Good insurance really can step in and help you in an emergency. Insurance saved my butt a time or two over the years for things that I could have never anticipated. Like the time, three years after renovating a home, termites showed up and the home owner decided to blame the renovator. Essentially, be prepared because trees will topple over, floods and fires will happen, and people will trip and fall. Insurance and a great attorney will protect your business from crashing due to a petty lawsuit. It is sad to say, but we truly live in a world full of frivolous lawsuits.

Principles That Work

Business is about honor in relationships. However, don't misunderstand: Relationships are necessary, but insufficient within themselves. You must also have a competitively priced product and a unique approach to how you provide your service. You *must* figure out a way to distinctly promote your product. Just as most people won't buy from someone they don't trust no matter how good the products are, neither would they continue to buy inferior products from a friend. For example, if you're a real estate agent, your clients will not come back to you and they will not send you their friends and family if you don't take good care of them. If you're a life coach, they will not renew. If you sell cars, they will not come back to you for their next car. Providing great customer service is the key to repeat business, and for goodness sake, if you're going to be an entrepreneur, approach your business with a long-term perspective. Don't take advantage of a client today for a quick buck. Do right by your client, and you'll find that your clients will do right by you. They will help you grow your business.

- **Give to Get:** To succeed in business, you must first think of giving, not taking. If you give your customer value in products and service, you'll get repeat business. If you take care of your employees, they'll value their jobs and take good care of your customers. If you pay your vendors on time, they'll expedite a rush order for you. The principle of reciprocity is so basic to relationships that even an enemy is likely to shake your hand if you reach out. Everyone is more willing to help a nice guy. You can develop this important attitude by making sure whatever you do with others constitutes a fair exchange.

- **To Lead is to Serve:** Invariably, the most successful people are those who manage to make the transition from being a doer to being a manager and a leader. Most of us are trained as skillful doers. To maximize our full potential, we have to learn how to motivate people. Leaders could get away with tyranny in the old days when people were concerned about meeting their basic needs for physical security, food, and shelter. Today's employees, however, will not tolerate authoritarian leadership. They want job satisfaction and the opportunity to develop self-esteem through their work. They want to build relationships, feel significant, and feel accomplished on a weekly basis. They want to be successful, to do something worthwhile, and to work for a company that has a sense of purpose and a mission. Today's employees perform best when they have a supportive and friendly place to work. Thus, a leader takes on the function of serving more than supervising. His or her main responsibility is to make sure employees have the tools they need and an environment they can succeed in. Think of yourself as a teacher, helping people get their job done, sharing your experiences, and making sure you maintain a culture many people will subscribe to. Then your people will want to work hard and perform to the best of their ability. You can develop your leadership skills by playing a supportive role to the people who report to you now.

- **Openness is Expansion:** Because business is about transactions and people dealing with people, an important business skill is the ability to develop a rapport with people quickly. People always appreciate you reaching out to make a connection with them. The key is to remove the barrier, which is the discomfort of the unknown, and search for common ground, whether it be sports, children, fishing, or your favorite bands. Emotional intelligence is being aware of one's emotions and knowing how to handle interpersonal relationships.

Emotional intelligence has been proven to be more valuable to leaders than a tremendously high IQ. It is the key to both personal and business success. Tell people about yourself, and ask good questions about them. Ensure that they do most of the talking as a result of your great questions. Give thought to your questions, and please do not forget to listen to their answers. Do not only half listen, formulating your response while they're answering your questions. To do so only lowers your emotional intelligence score, and people around you can feel it. People used to talk to each other on airplanes and such. Now they typically avoid it at all costs. Don't be afraid to share your family stories, business secrets, and your methods of doing things. You can learn from others by opening up and sharing about yourself. If you aren't open and responsive, new relationships are slow in developing. It takes confidence to be open, and that confidence takes time to build. Although openness can make you vulnerable, it will create many opportunities. You may occasionally lose some things by being open, but you will gain so much more in return.

- **Be Honest:** Honesty really is the best policy. Be honest with your customers. A customer is more likely to buy from you if he/she trusts you because they perceive less risk. Your honesty provides the foundation for that trust. Be honest with your employees. It makes your life simpler in the long run. For example, if you truthfully state the mission of your business, people who support that mission will join you, and those who don't will go somewhere else. This way, you end up with people around you that are happier and, thus, more productive. Selling many homes and other various things through my journey I've learned a very important lesson about being honest with myself. At night, in my bed, when the lights are out, if I recall a wrong committed for my own selfish reasons, I'll take that time to reflect and give it serious consideration. Sometimes, I'll go and change or adjust whatever it was, and other times it's just too late. I was selfish, and I realize it in reflection. I must forgive myself and sometimes ask God to forgive me as well. Outside of that, the morning is a new day. Leave yesterday's mistakes behind you and choose today to be honest, honor people, and create win-wins with integrity. In addition, be honest with yourself about your limitations. Doing so takes confidence. Each of us is unique. Our skills are different, and what we're willing to do is different. By accepting yourself as you are, you can set reasonable business goals, make better business decisions, and keep your ego from getting in the way.

- **Be Open to Change:** Many people are facing early retirement or entering an uncertain job market. This time may provide an important growth opportunity for you. Without change, there is no growth. If you don't embrace growth, you may miss out on progressive steps in your journey. The change you face may be difficult, but it just might be the best thing that has happened to you.

- **Know Yourself:** The first step in understanding others is to understand yourself. One way you learn about yourself is by dealing with difficult people and difficult situations. In that process, you reflect upon yourself to gain new insight. Dealing with difficult people is hard work, but self-knowledge is your reward. There is huge value in embracing the ongoing reality of knowing yourself. Maybe you never realized the level of anger you're capable of if someone were to steal from your business. That would be good to know about yourself, right? Reaching out, getting involved, and helping people may be the best way to prepare yourself for business. Perhaps the best way to learn about yourself is to show compassion for others. By helping others solve their problems, you may better learn your limitations and come to understand your own problems with greater depth. Empathy becomes a mirror to yourself.

- **Always Learn, Learn, and Learn Some More:** You should always be willing to learn and not shut down your brain. Our brains are like sponges, and most of us seem to only want to learn about people's successes but not their failures. This is a huge mistake. By limiting yourself to information, you only get a partial view of how that individual succeeded in the first place. When you're first starting out, you should be willing to read anything and everything so as not to make stupid mistakes, including huge money losses and wasted time. This can be avoided if you just take some time to open your eyes and listen to people. You need to be on top of your game in any given situation, whether that's going to a meeting or presenting your idea to obtain angel investors. You should always be prepared to learn. Education abounds online, both free and paid. All new technologies can be researched, studied, and applied to your business. Study other fields, not just your own. You should hunger for knowledge and wisdom on a daily basis just as you hunger for food, clothing, sex, and sleep.

- **Be the Best at What You Do or Surround Yourself With the Best People:** "Be the best at what you do" is a common answer given by wealthy people when asked *how* they are so wealthy. Of course being the best at what you do goes hand-in-hand with doing what you love; however, being the best at something really takes dedication. Many rich people have said that in order to survive and have financial freedom, you must plot your idea from A to B in the sense that point A is where you are now, and point B is what you are trying to achieve and where you want to be in five years. Never forget your main aim and the objective of your business. Once you find something you want to do, in order to survive and become financially free in the future, you must be the best at it. Being a serial entrepreneur has caused me to let my muscles weaken in some areas. My grandfather used to say, "Jack of all trades, master of none." He referred to himself as such and it seems I have also unintentionally landed there by spreading my efforts, interests, and investments into different arenas.

Being good at a lot of things and not having mastered any particular thing can be frustrating both for me and for those around me, but I've accepted that being a jack of all business trades and a master of none is okay with me. Thus, surrounding myself with people who possess clear, strong gifts is the only way I can compensate for my weaknesses.

- **"I Can't" or "I Don't" Will Not Help You Survive:** It's not enough for you to say, "I have this great idea, but I don't have any money, so I'm not going to do it," or "I have money saved up, but I don't want to risk it." Taking a risk is a must in life. Entrepreneurs must evaluate the risk and and be willing to step out on a limb. Investing blood, sweat, and tears in the game to potentially make money is a real risk. You may potentially lose money as well. That is just as real. People who doubt themselves, people who push their desires and passions down year after year, and people who would rather keep the few thousand dollars they have already rather than risk it are the people who risk the disappointment of crushed dreams. Shattered dreams are real. They hurt. They break your expectations and perceptions. They shape your character. They sharpen your entrepreneurial sword. If you don't have money, there are several things you can do. You can work for a few years and save the needed resources, always planning your idea until then. Save wisely and regularly. You can take a small amount of money and begin to do on a small scale what you are dreaming of doing on a bigger scale. Start small, and then healthy things grow! Or, you can start networking and obtain investments. Or, you can find a partner and bootstrap the business. One puts in the money and the other puts in the work, or they share in both. There are a lot of ways to achieve and get started. "I can't" is a defense mechanism made out of being scared of failure when presented with a risky investment opportunity. Can you imagine if Bill Gates had said, "I can't build a computer," or Mark Zuckerberg said, "I can't build Facebook"? However, they took the risk. They could have easily failed and been left unemployed. Instead, they are both currently billionaires, and many folks, like myself, made a great return on investment when we bought their stock early on or when they had the early dips. They became wealthy yes, good for them, but guess what? They made me wealthier because I chose to buy their stock on the public market. How many thousands of people did they make wealthier and how many college savings accounts went up tremendously because of their stakes in Facebook?

- **In Order to Survive, You Must Be Fit:** This is meant literally, but it plays well with my Fit Realty brokerage. You have to sleep sufficiently for your body. If that is six hours or eight hours, only you can determine how much and what type of sleep is best for your body and mind. Food really is a huge deal and cannot be underestimated. For example, if you have an allergy with gluten, milk, or various nuts and you aren't aware of the allergy, your body is probably telling you, but you aren't connecting the dots. Also, a lot of people don't make time to exercise consistently. Without health, you won't survive long term or be able to stay the course. It would be sad to become ill before you reach your dreams. Take a break. Have a sabbath. If you are able, take a sabbatical of two to six months minimum. I haven't yet been able to do that, but I hear it's lovely and significant. I do hope to achieve that goal for myself one day as well. None of us becomes immune to death just because we make some money, become wealthy, and have many properties. Sickness, disease, and death are all real risks to your business success, and more importantly to your personal health and wellness. We must not forget that stress is easily invoked, and although stress can be a good motivator to meet our deadlines and do our work, it can also be bad in excess. We mustn't forget to treat ourselves once in a while also. This doesn't have to be extravagant. It can be going out with a couple of friends and even to networking events, which would be beneficial to both your business and helping improve your social life.

- **Survival Always Changes, So You Have to Adapt:** If you look back at prehistoric times, you'll see survival of the fittest literally meant the fittest, that is, the strongest, the best with tools, and the best with weapons. Back then, people had had to hunt for their own food. Fast forward to today, and survival is something else entirely. Now, the challenge is to constantly adapt to new technology. For example, businesses have gone from simple brick and mortar to having an online presence. It's also critical for businesses to be mobile friendly. For example, ninety percent of our real estate leads are generated from mobile devices, which is not how it was even just a few short years ago. Most of us have had to adapt to survive and make money. If you look at eBay, for example, they were the first e-commerce business online, and by adapting quickly to the changes of technology and society, they were able to create a multibillion-dollar company. Always be anticipating what's likely to happen next in terms of making money and surviving then be the first to exploit that gap. The first mover's advantage is very real in entrepreneurship. Executing a fast plan as markets shift can be very rewarding. Some technology, for example, that used to cost millions of dollars is now available as an app on your phone for less than ten dollars.

In the end, it's vitally important for aspiring entrepreneurs to remember this: whether you have great talents or little talents, great wealth or no wealth, if you continue creating and maintaining good daily, weekly, and yearly habits, you will be successful. Success is defined as the ongoing accomplishment of worthwhile goals. One of those goals may be to raise a family. This doesn't have an end point, but can have incremental accomplishments along the way, year over year, month over month. Don't wear yourself out to become rich. Show discretion and choose to embrace the journey of today, not waiting to enjoy life only when you reach some perceived goal you have in mind. Legendary basketball coach John Wooden says it's a matter of satisfaction, "Success is peace of mind, which is a direct result of self-satisfaction in knowing you did your best to become the best you are capable of becoming."

CHAPTER 3

NO PERFECT SPOUSE, NO PERFECT HOUSE:
BUYING YOUR FIRST HOME

I believe real estate is hands down the best investment there is. Residential single-family homes or townhouses, commercial buildings, or storage properties, if purchased and managed well, can provide long-term income for the owner. My role model in this regard is my father. From the start of his marriage to my mother, my dad would purchase small, beat-up homes and renovate them himself, putting in all of the physical work with the guidance of his father. While he worked for a glass factory, he would repair one or two properties at a time, eventually accumulating a handful of rental properties. These properties led to other investment opportunities for him. I remember as a child riding around after church with my dad looking for businesses for sale. Eventually, he found a plumbing company that was for sale. It had three part-time employees, two run-down vans, and some basic equipment. After purchasing the company out of bankruptcy, he took a risk and quit his job at the glass factory. He had his employees teach him what he needed to know about plumbing. The passive income from his rental properties is what helped financially sustain our family until the plumbing business became profitable. He was eventually able to purchase a storage-unit facility, which became another source of income. Because of these real estate investments, he has been able to retire well and enjoy his golden years collecting rent checks, playing pickleball and shuffleboard, and swimming in sunny Florida.

Real estate ownership has paved the way for wealth and business startups more than any other industry in history. There's wealth to be gained from buying and selling homes, flipping homes, and passing along real estate through generations of families. Real estate has also been used for home equity lines for people to start their business as seed or start-up capital. Some people have even lived in a home for two years or more, sold it for a big profit, kept the entire profit tax-free, and used the money to open a restaurant. Real estate is, in most cases, a big influencer on the ground floor of success. A foundation of wealth for the majority of Americans was created through real estate property.

Getting a foot on the real estate ladder can be challenging; daunting even. Making the decision to buy your first home is a massive life experience and requires a lot of careful planning and thought. Your first adventure into the world of real estate can be scary. Buying your first home represents the beginning of a new chapter in your life. Most people are aware of the commitment, the financial impact, and the life changes that usually accompany buying a house, but some don't realize there are a lot of emotions involved. Many of the decisions made during the home-buying process that people end up regretting are fueled by strong feelings rather than sound logic or rational thinking. It's extremely important to stay in control and avoid letting your emotions drive your decisions when buying your first house. There are many professionals out there to help ease the stress of the process. A real estate agent can help find the right house for the season of life you're in.

Despite the potential stress involved, many people find the prospect of looking for a new house thrilling. Different neighborhoods, the number of bedrooms and bathrooms, and square footage are topics one might begin to investigate. Features of a home, such as granite countertops, stainless steel appliances, and wood floors are what some might include in their search options on the internet. It's a fun process for a lot of people, and many will watch their favorite HGTV home-hunting show with a whole new mindset. A few years ago, our real estate team was featured on a HGTV show finding someone the perfect home. It was quietly humorous to me as I watched the show knowing the real story of what happened throughout the buying and closing process. The show, of course, didn't air the less-than-glamourous aspects. Just a reminder that buying a house, just like all parts of the journey of life, won't be as attractive as seen on TV.

You may not be a list-making kind of person, but in the case of buying a home, it's imperative for you to separate what you want from what you need. Having a list of the things you need will automatically eliminate some properties so you don't waste your time. A list of wants is something that can go either way, but they're things you can live without. This could be location, an open-concept home, stairs that don't directly face the door, curb appeal, a large backyard, no busy street, and/or close to highways and shopping. You may have to sacrifice a large yard for that third bedroom.

Take the Emotion Out of Buying Your First Home

Bring an objective person with you when you're house hunting. If you get excited by restaurant-style kitchens, spa bathrooms, entertainment rooms, etc., bring an impartial person with you. They'll make sure you stay on budget and ask questions such as, "Are those real hardwood floors?" It's a great way to stay present and look beyond the surface of a house. It would be nice if a seller would paint the walls a neutral color before listing their home, but this doesn't always happen. Painting is easy, and you can do it yourself or hire professionals. Changing carpet is cheap, yet many people pass on a whole house due to the carpet color or wear and tear. A great real estate agent can possibly even get that negotiated into the purchase if it's important to you and you're tight on money. Just as body parts sag with age, homes wear out with age. That's okay. The key is knowing what the expensive repairs will be that could later create a true financial burden you aren't confident you could handle down the road. If the roof is getting really, really worn and ripping, that may be a deal killer for you, or it could be an affordable fix that you don't think much of when the time comes.

Your tastes may be different from a home seller. You and the seller may both enjoy granite countertops, but there are many colors from which to choose. A seller may like dark colors, and you may prefer light colors. You may like modern cabinetry in a light color; a home seller may prefer modern cabinetry in a dark color. These are cosmetic changes that are easy to fix. Keep this in mind and don't write off a home because you don't like the kitchen cabinets. You could be missing out on a fantastic home. Realize that cosmetic changes, like hardware and paint, are easy fixes. Leave your emotions at home and view homes through an objective lens. You can always remodel and make the home what you want it to be. The caveat is to remember that one day you may want to sell your home. Take into consideration that what you like, a future home buyer may not. Obviously, you want to make your home your own, but you must also think about resale value as you make your remodeling decisions.

Common Fears of Buying a Home

Buying property is a major investment, both financially and emotionally. So it's no wonder some people are a little bit scared. Fear is a powerful human emotion. Be bold and take a risk. Even if you're the first person in your family to own a home, trust that it's a worthy goal and step into home ownership. Below are some common fears that can stop you from making the leap into the property market and what you can do to solve them.

- **Fear of Over Paying:** Many properties don't have accurate price guides and are listed for sale by inexperienced agents or for sale by owner, where the owner prices the house at what they dream it's worth due to their emotional connection. Buyers often worry they're taking a stab in the dark when it comes to prices. Some buyers become overcautious, spend far too long researching in a moving market, and end up in an analysis paralysis where they become unable to make a decision. The only way to overcome this fear is through diligent market research. Take price guides as just that, do your own sales research, and seek independent advice from the experts. However, don't get bogged down in too much research and miss out on what could be the right property. You should also trust your gut and choose to pay what you feel comfortable with if the asking price and your budget are good. With or without good comparable sales, you may just want to pull the trigger; I've rarely been disappointed buying something I felt was a great deal.

- **Fear of Buying the Wrong Property:** The property market is full of uncertainties, and a fear of missing out on the "right" or "perfect" property is very common among buyers. People wonder if it's better to buy a smaller house closer to the city or move further away to get a bigger piece of land or a bigger house. Is it better to buy a house to renovate or a house with recent upgrades? And which suburbs are going to do better? It's advisable that buyers sit down and really map out a strategy for their property purchase. What stage of life are you in? What are your short-term personal and family goals? What is really important to you? It boils down to understanding your priorities. Most people have to compromise when buying a property. That is part of the fun on the journey. There is no perfect decision and no perfect house.

- **Fear of Selling Agents/Buyers Agents:** The process of buying a property can be overwhelming for certain buyers, like those entering the property market for the first time or those who have had a bad experience with an agent. As much as I enjoy the TV shows that feature real estate agents as the main characters, they do add to the negative view of agents. Some people feel that real estate agents are not very transparent and worry that they'll get tricked or blindsided in the process. There are good and bad, weak and strong, honest and dishonest real estate agents. That is just a hard fact. Choosing wisely is important. On the other hand, don't be paranoid or you'll sabotage all agent relationships. There are thousands of caring and knowledgeable real estate agents across each state and region. Familiarize yourself with local agents, and you'll soon start to see the way they operate and how they differ, and you'll become more confident in dealing with them.

- **Fear of a Bubble or Crash:** We all want to have a crystal ball that can predict the future, particularly when it comes to the property market, where many buyers speculate about sharp rises or fear a bubble or crash. Some buyers are concerned they're buying at the peak of the market and paying premium prices and that the market might collapse entirely. Or, if the economy turns bad, jobs might be lost and mortgages can't be repaid. While investors might want to time a purchase carefully by watching the market, others might not need to worry quite so much. If you're buying a home you plan on living in for many years, the state of the market is less of a concern compared to the importance of timing your purchase with when you're financially and emotionally ready. The best time to buy is when you're ready. The focus should be to buy a solid property that will do well in the long run, rather than worry about market blips. If interest rates go up, no worries; you've already locked in your rate. If interest rates go down, no problem; you can always refinance. Don't overthink, and don't succumb to fear.

- **Fear of Missing Out:** The most emotional of all property fears is the intangible fear of missing out. This can cause serious inaction in many buyers. Many buyers worry that the perfect property is just around the corner and they'll miss out if they buy now. When you're buying a property, you're buying at a given point in time. Buyers should not dwell on what has already sold or what may or may not come on the market next week. That's a futile exercise. The best you can do is make sure you have thoroughly covered the entire existing market. I literally had buyers on the way to their closing who wanted to look at another house just to see the one that got away. They had already done a home inspection and appraisal and had a U-Haul. The grass is not greener on the other side. Even if it is, make a decision and move forward. If your timing isn't perfect, most likely the market growth will make it right in the end when it comes time to sell. As you're chasing greener grass, the interest rates are rising. Choose a good agent and a knowledgeable local market loan officer when possible. Then, walk with confidence, ask good questions, and enjoy the ride!

Builder Inventory Versus Custom Built Versus Re-Sale New Homes

You might imagine the experience of buying your dream home as starting with an empty lot, picking out every feature from the layout of the floorplan to the color of the drapes, and then settling in to wait while your home is built completely from scratch. It's a time-honored process that works wonders for many. However, what if you don't have months to spare waiting for ground-up construction on your new home? Easy! Buy an inventory home. Also known as quick move-in homes or speculative (spec) homes, inventory homes are either already under construction or completely built by the time you enter the picture, meaning you can purchase a brand-new home and enjoy the luxury of a faster move-in time.

- **Builder Inventory Homes:** There are two primary advantages to buying an existing new construction home: timeframe and cost. Once you're pre-approved by your lender, you can shop around, pick out a home, and make an offer. A qualified real estate agent can streamline the process by helping you find appropriate properties, guiding you through negotiations, and assisting with the paperwork. Once your offer is accepted, you may be able to close and move in within a month or two. Many builders will allow you to choose some of the final options if you put the property under contract before it's finished. For example, it is very common for a builder to let you choose carpet color, tile, countertop color, and sometimes even light fixtures. This will depend on the builder and on the stage of the home. Also, builders often roll out many inventory/spec homes, which means they build a house and hope someone likes and buys what they built. Because of this large volume of homes, which have minimal customizations, the same five to ten models are built hundreds and hundreds of times per year. This process and approach can make buying a new home cheaper than custom building a home.
- **Custom-Built New Homes:** Building a custom new home doesn't offer some of the same convenience as buying an existing house or an already built new home. You will need to locate custom builders in your region. You should ask the builders or builder agents you contact what land they have or what land they know about that you may be able to buy and have them build

on, or if the builder owns it and will build a custom home for you on that land. Not only do you have to find the land, you also have to factor in the time to find an architect or builder with floorplans you like, and you have to choose every element of the new structure. In addition, you have to be sure the land is buildable and that the home will fit according to city zoning and building codes. Joining an existing development can streamline the process, though it may limit your degree of choice. In this situation, if you can locate a truly gifted builder who has a streamlined home-building system, your limitations are in many ways taken off and you can customize to your budget and heart's content. The biggest advantage of a custom-built home is you are much more likely to get exactly what you want. For many, this factor alone is enough to choose building over buying, but there are other advantages too. A new home is more efficient, especially with the new energy codes, including better HVAC (heating, ventilation, and cooling), insulation, and air filtration standards. Better efficiency is good for the environment and can save you money on your utility bills each month. Another perk? A new house may literally be physically better for you. A new home is less likely to have the health concerns or toxic materials of an older home with things such as asbestos, lead paint, mold, etc. A new home can be built with certain materials, making it better for the environment. Energy Star-rated appliances and efficient toilets, plumbing fixtures, and electrical fixtures allow you to build "green" for a more sustainable home in the long run. Also, you have the option to install and/ or wire for future technological upgrades, such as home automation and solar upgrades. The biggest drawbacks to custom building a home tend to be the higher costs and longer timeframe, both of which can increase throughout the home-building process. That said, you can limit the risk that your house will go over budget or take longer than you expected by working with a reputable builder and having a good contract in place. Have your potential builder provide references and then check their past homeowner references. To avoid unexpected price increases, try to use a lump sum contract instead of a cost-plus contract. A lump sum contract specifies a fixed price for construction, putting the risk of costs running over on the builder instead of the buyer.

Buying a Re-Sale Home

A lot of people prefer buying existing re-sale homes, which are easy to find in every city and every county in our country. They can also be easier to finance. An existing home may be a better option if you would like to be in a particular established neighborhood near work, school, friends, and/or family. Also, odds are that the home will have mature landscaping, so you won't have to worry about starting a lawn, planting shrubs, and waiting for trees to grow. If you want to live close to town, your best bet will be an existing home since most, if not all, of the land will have already been built upon. On the flip side, the biggest disadvantage of buying an existing home may be that you may not get exactly what you want. You may not be in love with the floor plan. You may wish that the half-bath on the first floor were a full bath or that there was another bedroom on the main floor. An otherwise beautiful four-bedroom house may only have one bathroom, or the kitchen may be too small with no room for expansion. Unless you find an existing home that has exactly what you want and is in perfect condition, you will have to spend additional money on remodeling, repairs, decorating and/or landscaping. These additional expenses should be factored into the overall price, especially when choosing among various properties and comparing the cost to building your own house.

Pros and Cons of Buying a Re-Sale Home:

- **Pro:** There is no need to wonder what the house will look like.
- **Pro:** There is little to no worry regarding the interior of the house, as everything needed is already there, and all that's left to do is arrange, paint, and decorate.
- **Pro:** Buying an existing home generally takes less time than building a new one.
- **Pro:** There are more location choices with a re-sale home in a neighborhood or school system you may want to be in.
- **Pro:** Buyers often have more room for negotiating the price point or terms of sale than with new homes.
- **Con:** The internal condition of the home can be a concern. When buying a home, the potential buyer can check out the house from all views and angles yet may not be able to check between the walls, under the

floorboards, or inside the ceiling, where it matters most. Unseen deterioration due to pests and insects could be cause for concern.

- **Con:** Re-sale homes will have older plumbing, electric, roof, insulation, etc.
- **Con:** Buyers can usually purchase a larger home with the same amount of money with a re-sale than with new construction.

Pros and Cons of Buying a Newly Constructed Spec Home/Standing Inventory:

- **Pro:** There is a warranty that each builder is required by state law to provide the home buyer. Virginia, for example, requires a one-year doorknob to doorknob and five-year structural warranty. Know your rights and find a builder who backs their product. You also will have manufacturer warranties for appliances, heating, AC, etc.
- **Pro:** The enjoyment in choosing exactly what goes into a new home, architecture, materials, trim and light packages can be a rewarding experience in itself.
- **Pro:** A major advantage of buying or choosing a new home is having everything brand new. It provides peace of mind, especially in terms of stability with all new foundation, secure walls, new insulation, etc.
- **Pro:** New homes typically feature modern architecture and layouts, such as great rooms, bigger closets, and additional bathrooms. These built-in conveniences are handy.

- **Con:** Purchasing a new home will generally cost more money per square foot than buying an existing property in the same zip code/region.
- **Con:** It will generally take longer to move into a new home built from the ground up versus buying an existing home.
- **Con:** Buyers normally have more opportunity to negotiate both the terms and the price when buying a re-sale home. New homes are typically not very negotiable.
- **Con:** If you like a more traditional layout with a formal living room and dining as your preference, those layouts may not be regularly offered.

Pros and Cons of Building a Custom Home:

- **Pro:** Custom homes have all of the same pros as new construction standing inventory homes mentioned above.
- **Pro:** You get to choose your location. When custom building, you're looking for a piece of land that will fit your dream or a piece of land that's so amazing you will want to reshape the home design to fit the land.
- **Pro:** You get a custom floorplan. You can choose your home model and placement of each room and any unique areas, such as a room with a bar or an insulated office space to block out the noise of children when working from home. Handicap accessibility is an enormous pro of a custom new home.
- **Pro:** You get to choose your architectural exterior design, including colors, trim packages, fixtures, etc.

- **Con:** Locating quality buildable and affordable land may prove to be really challenging depending on the region in which you live. Specific neighborhood or school zones may be particularly challenging to find the right buildable lot for your dream home.
- **Con:** In choosing your custom location, there are challenges to be prepared for, including city zoning, water, sewer, and electric approval, and concerns of building on environmentally protected areas.
- **Con:** Unexpected surprises resulting in building delays aren't rare. The builder could run into wetlands, permitting issues, city water and sewer taps versus septic and well. These may cause delays while building your dream home. If you chose a good builder, just be patient and understand these challenges do arise on occasion.
- **Con:** Quality custom builders are few and far between. Having a trustworthy builder goes a long way. Each region is unique. Choose wisely, and you'll avoid this con all together.

Even if you start your home search set on finding the perfect existing property, you may end up deciding to build to get exactly what you want. Conversely, you may plan on building and later decide an existing home is a better fit. In either case, working with a qualified and experienced professional, whether that's a real estate agent or a general contractor, can help ensure the process goes as smoothly as possible.

Understanding the Value of a Property as a Homeowner

As a homeowner or an early investor, you must be willing to go all the way and get your hands dirty, digging up any necessary information on what you are about to put your money into. Do some research on and off the internet. Call a local title company for advice. The internet can be a great starting place to look for information; however, not all data obtained from the internet is 100% accurate. Therefore, it's safer to gather data from multiple sources.

- **Get Information from Multiple Sources:** You can get information from several agencies; you just need to know what kind of information you seek and where to get it. Licensed real estate agents have plenty of experience in your area and are aware of recent sales, even if they didn't make the sale. Contact realty offices and see if there are agents willing to talk about recent sales. Remember to get all the necessary information about the sale, including at least the selling price, date of sale, square footage, year built, and number of bedrooms and bathrooms. It would probably make the real estate agent more willing to share information with you if they see you as a potential client. Local governments keep records of recent property sales, which are usually held in the tax assessment office. Contact the office and see if they can give you a list with all the details of each property, including selling price, date of sale, square footage, year built, and the number of bedrooms and bathrooms. You need all of this information to make a good guess on the market price for the home you plan to buy. Insurance companies also keep data on real estate sales in a given area. Some will provide you with a property profile for free, hoping you'll buy insurance from them. The property profile will contain a list of comparable properties specific to the aspects you're interested in. Note that not all companies will do this for free, but you might still be able to obtain a property profile for a small fee. Local newspapers are resourceful too. Town, city, and county newspapers often publish information on local property sales. You can scan the real estate section for information on recent sales. Bear in mind that you might not get all of the information you need solely from a newspaper. You'll probably still have to contact a tax assessor or real estate agent or other source, like the ones mentioned above, for all of the necessary information. Consider the old-fashioned style: Talk to neighbors to find out more about the property. However, if you know you already have a power team in place that includes a real estate company, a mortgage company, and an insurance company, then you may not need to seek the advice of many others. Technology has made it so that real estate agents can provide tremendous amounts of quality data in a very short time.

- **Comps:** Short for housing comparables, "comp" is a common term used by agents and appraisers when comparing home sales nearby. Comps are a way to help you figure out what a home is worth based on the recent sales prices of similar properties in the area. Home sellers use comps to help them determine an asking price, while buyers can use comps to decide how much to offer. As such, it's an important concept for both buyers and sellers to master. Some local governments and realty sites publish information about the area on their websites. An online search engine is a good first step to take before you make any phone calls or visit any offices. That way, you can get an idea of what information is available without a lot of inconvenience. Keep in mind that new construction homes appraise differently than regular re-sales. If you put a brand new, 2,500-square-foot, two- or three-story home in an old dilapidated neighborhood, the new home will be compared to other new homes within about a three-mile radius if needed. Organize all of the information you've gathered and make comparisons. Consider the pros and cons and check the facts. Finally, determine what it's worth to you before you put your money on it. When you check online for homes that are for sale on the different types of sites mentioned above or any other realty site, you're likely to see the price range of similar homes in the area that sold recently. Keep in mind that a sale older than six months won't tell you much. In fact, some lenders only look at transactions within the past three months when it's appraisal time. It's much easier in a hot market with a lot of sales or comps to choose from. On the other hand, in a slower market, when the home has excellent amenities, you will have a harder time finding comps. For example, if you're interested in a house that has a lake view where houses almost never come on the market, finding certain comps will be a challenge. There are multiple factors to take into consideration when looking at comps.

- **Property Type:** If you're evaluating a single-family home, then your comps need to be single-family homes of similar size and room counts. If you're evaluating an apartment building, then you should choose comps that have a similar number of units. If you're evaluating an office building, then look at office buildings of similar size, quality, and class.

- **Transactional Factors:** What is the home's worth according to the appraiser? Please note, this number can be close to or very different from current sales prices and market values depending on how recently they assessed properties, property-specific exemptions (or the norm for the area), and the speed at which prices are changing.

- **Amenities:** Amenities, including a pool, a spectacular view, a guest house, a patio, a fireplace, etc., add to the value of a home.

- **Buyer's Choice:** Individual choices differ and contribute to how much value a home and its surroundings have to the buyer. Does the size, style, number of rooms, safety, age, or amenities suit your needs?

- **Location:** Location is one of, if not *the* biggest determinant of a property value. When it comes to location, quite a number of factors need to be considered, including, but certainly not limited to, convenience to work, shopping, and interstates, potential growth in the area, and redevelopment.

- **Age:** Houses built around the same time usually have similar amenities. Remodeling usually alters the design, but some counties include an "adjusted year built" designation to account for major remodels or updates.

- **Other Important Considerations:** Consider purchasing a home in an area where the value of real estate purchases has been steadily increasing over time. It's risky to purchase a home in an area where the value of real estate has seen wild fluctuations or downward trends. Consider your investment. As much as you'd like to pay less for higher value, you need to treat your home as an investment. It's important to purchase a home where its value appreciates. Location, location, location remains the cornerstone of a good real estate decision.

  Consider the possibility of easier access to good educational institutions, healthcare services, recreational opportunities, and other community amenities. The condition and proximity of everything from parks to doctors' offices to sporting facilities will potentially have an impact on the value of a home.

  Consider access to local transportation links. Easy access to major roads and highways, as well as public transportation options, all contribute to the value of a home and comfort for the occupant. You may be interested in walkability and public transit. You can check on a home you are considering buying online by entering the address into WalkScore.com. This site rates neighborhoods based on access to public transit and proximity to services and amenities. However, keep in mind that a home located too close to noisy rail lines, freeways, and high-traffic areas will not fetch top dollar during resale and will also have its share of discomforts. Accessible transportation links is desirable; direct adjacency to noisy transportation/infrastructure is not.

- **Hire an Appraiser:** Finally, in an effort to determine the value of a property, you can always hire an appraiser to do the hard work. An appraiser will write an estimate of the property's market value by considering several factors regarding the home and the sales prices of other properties in the area. The appraiser bases part of the value of the home's condition by considering the property's location, age, number of bedrooms and bathrooms, square footage, and architectural features.

Steps to Buying Your Home

- **Find a Real Estate Agent You Trust:** The real estate profession is plagued by high turnover, which creates a workforce made up of a significant number of newcomers. Ensure that you opt for an agent with sufficient experience and familiarity with the area in which you are interested. Also, target an agent with the appropriate level of commitment and real estate education to act as your advocate throughout the house-buying process. Most importantly, interview at least three agents in person before finalizing your selection. Ask good questions to be sure there's experience to back up the big flashy promises. Not all brokerages are created equal. Not all real estate agents are equal. Some agents are much better than others and being completely aware of that is important in buying and selling homes.

- **Establish How Much You Can Pay for Your New Home:** First and foremost, set a budget and stick to it. There are numerous elements that go into determining how much you can afford to pay for your first home, including your earnings, your credit rating, your monthly expenses, your down payment, and your interest rate. Banks use various ratios to determine just how much you can borrow in acquiring your home. What is your comfort zone? If you've been approved for $300,000 and have a $30,000 down payment, you have up to $330,000 to spend on a home. How comfortable are you with spending $330,000? Find your comfort zone with the minimum and maximum amount you want to spend. Your agent also needs to have a good indication of your budget allowance. There is no point torturing yourself by looking at properties way out of your budget. Make sure you only view houses that you can actually afford. That monthly payment needs to be tolerable. Choosing to be house poor is not typically a good move. Your home should enhance your life, not be your monthly source of stress and financial burden.

- **Get Pre-Approved:** The first step in the pre-approval process would be to choose a loan officer or lender. Positive experiences from friends and family who have made recent home purchases can be taken into consideration, as well as recommendations from your real estate salesperson, who may have several lenders they've worked with in the past. Buyers, after choosing a loan officer or lender, get a pre-approval. When looking to buy a house, having a pre-approval from a lender will help ease the anxiety many people feel during the home-buying process. Knowing what you're approved to borrow and what's affordable for you narrows down the search from hundreds of houses to those that you can confidently walk in and say, Hey, we can really buy this. Let's put in an offer. The terms pre-approval and pre-qualification are often used interchangeably, yet they're very different from each other. With a pre-approval, the lender gives a written commitment of financing after obtaining bank statements, several years of tax returns, verification of employment, and a credit check from the buyer. While the process doesn't take a substantial amount of time, it does take more than its pre-qualification counterpart. A pre-qualification is the lender's prediction of what the buyer will qualify for based on the information that the buyer shares with them, but the lender probably doesn't verify this information. The risk with obtaining pre-qualification versus pre-approval is that the former can often lead to surprises in the future when a buyer formally applies for a mortgage.

- **Secure Funding:** The next step would be to decide what you want to pay and the selection of a type of loan product. While a lender will decide what you can borrow and which loan products are available to you, the buyer ultimately decides what they can afford and which mortgage products best fit their goals for a particular property purchase. Most lenders are very careful in their calculations, though they may not completely understand the subtleties of your spending habits, lifestyle, and what actually fits your family budget. It's wise for most buyers to leave room for both unexpected costs and expected expenditures such as furnishings, landscaping, and home repairs. Other conditions to obtaining funding would be an acceptable homeowner's insurance binder, continued creditworthiness and, in some cases (depending on the financing), proof of an acceptable home inspection. Title commitment occurs when all contingencies have been met. Financing is obtained at closing, when the documents are signed for the bank with a promise to repay. After obtaining pre-approval from a lender, there will still be a handful of conditions to meet before funds are released, including submitting an accepted purchase and sales contract to the lender and a satisfactory home appraisal. A lot of the upfront work that causes many buyers angst, though, has been completed.

- **Search for the Home Loan That is Right for You:** Searching and comparison shopping for a loan or mortgage loan will allow you to to acquire the best financing deal. A home finance loan, whether it is a home purchase, a refinance, or a home equity loan, is a product, just like a car, so the price and terms may be negotiable. You need to compare all of the fees involved in obtaining a home finance loan. Shopping, comparing, and negotiating may well save you thousands of dollars. You should also research to determine if you qualify for any of the variety of Federal Housing Administration loans or financing programs. For over 75 years, the FHA has assisted American homeowners. FHA housing programs and loans can assist you by providing mortgage insurance, which allows lenders to offer more attractive financing rates. FHA loans offer you low down payments, low closing expenses and, at times, less stringent credit qualifying. If you have served our country in the military, you may qualify for a VA loan. These provide 100% financing with no money down. This is possible because the VA backs the loan.

- **Make Sure You Understand Your Rights Through the Home-Buying Process:** Purchasing a house involves a significant financial outlay and must be considered carefully. The federal government has instituted a number of regulations to safeguard home buyers throughout the purchase process. The Real Estate Settlement Procedures Act (RESPA) is a federal law that helps protect shoppers from unfair practices by all the actors involved in the home buying and loan process. The Department of Housing and Urban Development enforces the Fair Housing Act and other federal regulations that prohibit discrimination as well as the intimidation of individuals in their houses. These laws cover virtually all housing in the United States and almost all housing transactions, including the rental and sales of housing units, plus the provision of mortgage loans. The issue of deceptive practices in the housing sector over the last decade has raised the profile of bad actors in the marketplace. Despite expanding access to capital for previously under-served borrowers, too many families are suffering due to the prevalence of abusive practices in some segments of the home-loan lending market. Both the federal government and state governments offer a variety of educational and counseling services. Consumer protection agencies have geared up to fight against deceptive and selfish business practices that have led to consumers feeling deceived.

- **Look for Programs in Your State to Help You Buy Your Home:** Many states have a Housing Finance Authority that offers a variety of programs for first-time home buyers. These programs often offer down-payment assistance and affordable fixed-income mortgage rates. The majority of programs are offered through private banks that operate in your state. Community banks and local credit unions are also worth exploring. Local banking has benefits when times get tough. I certainly learned that lesson during the 2007-2008 real estate market crash. Being respected members of a local bank was a true business saver during the great recession for my companies. The local banks that I was in a relationship with chose to let my partners and I continue to borrow money, build homes, and renovate homes even though financially we had become a high risk when property values plummeted. Our local banks honored their commitment to the community by allowing our businesses to continue to get the needed capital for growth. Not all builders and investors can say the same. Many banks around the country pulled their loans on builders, and, therefore, many builders went bankrupt rapidly.

- **Find the Home and Neighborhood That Meet Your Needs:** After laying the groundwork, now comes the fun part - finding the house and the neighborhood that meet your requirements. Your first home may not be your dream home. It may take two or three houses to finally get there, but you will eventually. Don't think that you necessarily have to spend all you have on your first home if it means you have to suffer in other areas of your life. Make the most of your real estate agent, as they can help educate you on what to look for and what to avoid, and they can provide you with reliable references for other experts you'll need along the way, such as inspectors and lenders. View as many houses in your price range and in your targeted location as you possibly can. Talk to friends and family about their real estate experiences, and really listen. People can pass on invaluable advice and recommend good professionals in the trade. Keep the faith that you'll find the right house for you. Wherever you go, keep an eye out for properties. The perfect house may just pop up and surprise you when you least expect it. However, don't forget: no perfect spouse, no perfect house! There is no such thing as a perfect house. Trust that the house you choose will be a great next step for you in this season of your life.

- **Negotiate to Get the Best Price:** When you're ready to make an offer on the house you love, get some advice from your buyer's agent. They know the market. As in all negotiations, it's significant to recognize who's operating from the position of most power. There are many market forces that can determine whether the buyer or seller of a home is in the best position, but it's usually the party with the best information that's operating with an advantage. Figure out your strategy based on your evaluation of the target home versus others and the general marketplace conditions. Any offer must also be contingent upon you obtaining financing and the house passing a professional property inspection. Working with the agent, a buyer will make an offer on a home to the seller. Once an offer has been accepted by a seller, the signed offer will be submitted to the lender as an accepted purchase and sale contract. This will initiate an appraisal of the home, which must be worth at least what the buyer and seller have agreed to and have no bank-required repairs.

When it comes to investment property, my dad and I negotiate very differently; personal residence is a different story. For an investment property, my father will stop by a house and make an offer that he thinks is fair. He doesn't base his offer on the asking price. He's patient and will wait someone out for weeks or months. More than once I have even seen him wait for years to get the property he has his eye on. I'm always amazed at how he will mention a property every now and then for a year or two, and then one day I find out he has obtained said property because my mom is all spun up, realizing she just got a new renovation job, which she loves to hate. For example, the asking price for a property may be $125,000. Dad decides he'll pay $40,000 for this future rental property. The owner will laugh. Six months later, Dad will have an agent send the same offer of $40,000. The owner will hesitantly say no. Six more months later Dad will send another offer of $40,000 and possibly add a note indicating he'll close with cash in two weeks and pay all costs of attorney closings. What do you know? Dad just obtained another rental property!

My negotiations are typically fast and furious. I tell a lot of back stories to prove my point. I may gather and compile facts on why the house is only worth $40,000 and try to sell the owner or the owner's agent on why they need to try to make the deal work. For me, if they do not accept my offer, I'll just move on and go to the next property. I'll forget that last deal and go for another, or I may put the old deal on the back burner and circle around in the style of my dad if the deal really keeps drawing me back. I'm not as patient as my father, but everyone is different, and various styles work equally well. There is more than one way to seal a deal.

- **Get All the Necessary Home Inspections:** Purchasing a house is probably the single largest purchase you will make in your lifetime, so you should be guaranteed that the property you want to get is in good condition. A property inspection is an evaluation of a home's situation by a trained expert. During a thorough house inspection, a certified inspector should take an in-depth and impartial look at the property you plan to purchase. It may behoove you to make the offer conditional on a home inspection. If the home has cracks in the foundation, has dangerous electrical wiring, or was poorly constructed, the inspector should be able to find this. They should also be able to locate mold, infestations, and water problems.

- **Shop for Homeowners Insurance to Protect Your New Home:** You may be able to save hundreds of dollars a year on homeowners insurance by doing a little comparison shopping. From increasing your deductible to confirming that you only insure what needs to be insured—your new dwelling and *not* the land underneath—you can save a bundle. Make sure you engage an insurance agent you can trust. Check with your agent and loan officer about the regional FEMA flood map and consider flood insurance even if it isn't required but you're concerned about the water flow in the area.

- **Complete the Closing and Settlement Process and Get Your Keys:** When closing day finally arrives, the hope would be you and your real estate agent show up at a predesignated location with a predesignated amount of money (if you need it for your down payment or closing costs). There, you're issued a title insurance policy, and you sign all of the necessary paperwork.

Weigh all of your options carefully. Remember the time you take when buying a home is a good investment. The time you invest will pay you back 100-fold during your lifespan, and what you can leave in knowledge and assets to your children or a favorite charity will help you and others make more money over the long haul.

CHAPTER 4

SHAKE THE WATER OFF YOUR DUCK FEATHERS:

BECOMING A SUCCESSFUL REAL ESTATE AGENT

The month that I turned in my doctorate dissertation was the same month I obtained my real estate license. That same month, I also sold my first house. I started selling houses every month, sometimes selling six to eight houses in a month by myself. Not too long after, I started a home-building business with my friend Kenton. For a short season, I spent a little more focus on the home building aspect than the real estate sales. When the market crashed, it was then that I knew I had to regroup and start a real estate team. Early on in my real estate agent team-building brokerage career, I only had five agents. I very distinctly remember standing outside the door before walking into a doctor's appointment one day and talking to my sales manager on the phone. I told her I wanted to grow the business to twelve agents. I had done the math all night and thought about the risks and the ups and downs with just five agents. I was convinced we needed to set our aim higher. She thought I was crazy. We were already having a hard time finding leads, managing various team issues that would arise, and keeping present sales volume stable for the five agents we had. However, with the goal in mind, some hard work and an entrepreneurial spirit, we were able to grow from five to twelve agents. Mastering lead creation became one of my passions, and we went from just a couple hundred leads each month to over one thousand leads a month during large lead/sale cycles. It was quite the journey in those couple of years. When we got to twelve agents, I knew we needed to grow to twenty. From twenty agents, we grew to thirty. We currently have fifity plus agents. The goal is to keep growing. Like my dad says, "healthy things grow." The way to do this, the way to stay healthy, is to empower more agents, more teams, and more brokerages to leverage our technology and agent services and grow themselves. I know that with a strong support staff, strong business systems, and strong business partners, we'll make it happen together.

Perhaps after purchasing your first home, learning so much about the process, and making your own dream come true, you might be interested in becoming an agent and helping others find their home. This is, in fact, why many people decide to become real estate agents. They are, essentially, dreamers helping dreamers.

Real estate agents must be confident, positive, and able to take things in stride, like water off a duck's back. When water hits the feathers of a duck, the natural oil in the feathers causes the perfect flow. There's no soaking in. It just rolls right off. Entrepreneurs, especially real estate agents, must learn to let certain things roll right off. I have said that to myself at least a million times in twenty years, especially when people laugh at my dreams, talk behind my back, plan against my companies, or attack me or my staff personally. When people throw their best spears at you, choose to let the words or actions affect you only as much as water hitting the feathers of a duck. If you just can't get past what others think, say or do to damage, attack, or abandon you and your dreams, then you may want to stop and ask yourself again if you really want to fight the battle of entrepreneurship and business.

Confidence as a Real Estate Agent

Top real estate agents are confident real estate agents. They know it's important to maintain a positive attitude to ensure their success. There are a number of ways to espouse confidence every day. From research to reactions, everything you do should be shaded with a positive attitude in order to impress real estate clients and to motivate yourself. Staying up to date on the real estate market can be a confidence booster. When you can speak to home sellers and buyers without having to pause to think or look up something, you come across as a knowledgeable professional. In addition to carrying out your own research to build your knowledge and boost your confidence, you can also work with other agents who can share new ideas and perspectives. Fill interactions with energy to make sure that confidence always comes across. A real estate agent should be excited about selling a home! That sort of attitude will impress clients as much as your thorough knowledge of the market or how to manage listings. Energy breeds confidence. Always remember to instill your daily real estate interactions with a dose of it. How does an agent effectively embrace excitement? By not sweating the small stuff! Tiny issues will always come up, but by not allowing them to ruin your day and instead maintaining a positive attitude, you can focus on improving your knowledge of your industry and take advantage of your excitement over deals. Small things can ruin the joy of the home buying or home selling experience if the real estate agent gets rattled at every turn. That's doing your client a disservice. Reach out to your broker advisors when needed, but don't drag your clients through every little drama of the journey. There's nothing more attractive than self-confidence. Use it to promote yourself professionally and succeed through all aspects of your life.

- **Repetition, Repetition, Repetition:** With all great athletes, practice is a necessity. If you have a player who can't catch the ball, what do you do? You have them practice catching the ball over and over for months until they develop the skill. The same mentality can be applied with improving your self-confidence. It's no surprise that experience is linked to self-confidence. It's something you often hear in the workplace. If there's something work-related that you aren't confident about, then work the system and practice it. Practice talking to clients and applicants or practice handling difficult situations. Don't let a negative response or rejection deter you from practicing. Embrace those negative experiences and appreciate the lessons they will undoubtedly teach you. This will help you better handle similar situations in the future. Persevere, and soon enough you'll be so confident you'll be able to handle any situation.

- **Stop the Negative Self-Talk:** We are all guilty of negative self-talk. It's that voice inside our head that immediately tells us what we just said was stupid. Or that voice that makes us overly aware of how we might have made a mistake. Learning self-awareness is very important. "Know thyself" is a challenge we should all pursue in life. The problem many of us have is that after we acknowledge our mistake, we need to simply forgive ourselves and shake it off, just like that water off a duck's back. Ruffle your feathers and move on, regardless of how big of a bucket of water gets thrown at you. Our negative self-talk brings us out of the present and distracts us from the work at hand. Professional athletes combat this by saying a positive mantra in their head. For Muhammad Ali, it was "I am the greatest." I have many Christian and Jewish friends who have scriptures memorized from the old and the new testaments, such as, "Therefore, do not throw away your confidence, which has a great reward. For you have need of endurance, so that when you have done the will of God you may receive what is promised," (Hebrews 10:35-36 ESV). Also, "But he said to me, 'My grace is sufficient for you, for my power is made perfect in weakness, Therefore, I will boast all the more gladly of my weaknesses, so that the power of Christ may rest upon me. For the sake of Christ, then, I am content with weaknesses, insults, hardships, persecutions, and calamities. For when I am weak, then I am strong," (2 Corinthians 12:9-11 ESV). A common Jewish encouragement is from King Solomon in Proverbs 24:16 HCSB, "Though a righteous man falls seven times, he will get up." If you have to, stand in front of the mirror at home, in the car, in the elevator, or in the bathroom every day and repeat these verses or mantras. Look at yourself and encourage yourself. By believing in yourself and reminding yourself of what makes you feel confident, whether it's a list of what you are proud of or a mantra, you can stay confident professionally.

- **Boost Your Confidence by Boosting Their Confidence First:** We all make mistakes and we all have self-doubt. While you should not point out your clients' weaknesses, make a point to compliment their strengths. Build their self-confidence as well. This can be as simple as complimenting your client's property upkeep or an applicant's handshake. By building others up, you will not only build a better relationship with your clients, but you will also be able to get out of your negative self-talk and focus on the present positive attributes.

- **Make Every Review a Positive One:** With confidence you can choose how to interpret feedback. While you shouldn't get carried away and completely ignore feedback from someone you trust, if you get negative and malicious feedback from an online review or an applicant, you have the power to decide if it's going to affect your self-confidence. Use negative feedback as constructive criticism, when it is valid, to grow as a professional and improve the way you interact with people. You'll have some haters; you'll get complaints. That's part of life for anyone in the service industry. Just remind yourself that the most you can do is get a little better each week, each month, and each year. That's all anyone can ask of any other fellow human. If it's a completely false accusation and you can't get the comment removed, don't dare let that hang over your head or let yourself believe it's going to sidetrack or wreck your career. It's really easy for many people to hide behind a screen and say nasty things.

- **Listen to Your Clients' Needs:** To earn the trust and confidence of your clients, you have to have a clear understanding of their needs. This involves more listening and less talking. Asking great questions is a noble life skill, and the better you get at it, the more it'll serve you and those around you. Home buyers are specific and know exactly what they're looking for in a house. Their perfect home may not exist, but if you listen and prioritize their wants, you can locate a property that's suitable for their family. When meeting with a new client, it's important to ask questions and get an idea of what they're looking for in a home, including square footage, number of bathrooms and bedrooms, bonus features, etc. Take notes and ask for clarification. Never assume anything. The level of interest you show builds their trust in your ability to find the right property. My absolute favorite part of being a real estate agent was the many hours in the car with clients and their families. I asked question after question, and we got to know one another. I understood their wants, needs, desires, and goals, both long and short term. It was one of the most enjoyable job roles I've had thus far in my life.

- **Don't Make Promises You Can't Keep**: Some buyers and sellers interview multiple agents before choosing one to work with. Since there's competition, you'll have to sell yourself and explain how you're better than other agents. Although you want to impress potential clients and gain their business, be careful about making promises you can't keep. Puffing or bragging is not uncommon or against the rules, but don't be that person who delivers inaccurate information due to being too lazy to go and look it up or to call the broker, etc. One of the fastest ways to lose the trust of your clients is not delivering on your promises. There are no guarantees in real estate. You cannot guarantee when or if a client's house will sell, and you cannot guarantee that a client will succeed in a bidding war. To gain new seller clients, some agents promise to sell their homes in 30 days at an extraordinarily high price. This might happen, but problems can arise if the home doesn't sell. The client might feel manipulated and choose to work with another agent. Confidence is good. Being overly confident can damage the relationship. Rather than making promises, mention the average length of time it usually takes to sell a home. Make it abundantly clear that there are no guarantees and that every case is unique.

- **Stay a Step Ahead of Your Client:** Some clients are savvy and have done their homework. They aren't real estate professionals, but they have a pretty solid idea of how the process works. For that matter, you need to stay a step ahead of these clients to prove you're working hard on their behalf. For example, if a client hasn't received any offers on their house after three or four weeks, or if the property isn't receiving many showings, don't wait for the client to suggest lowering the asking price. You make the suggestion! Additionally, you should actively search for properties that appeal to your buyer clients and bring these homes to their attention. Your clients shouldn't have to find their own properties. If your clients are always a step ahead, they could believe you aren't earning your commission. At the title closing table, a good agent wants their buyer or seller to be very pleased and to be able to say, "Yes, my agent did a great job." Set healthy expectations and cover your bases like a true professional. Strive to be a truly knowledgeable expert, not just someone who gets by. The reward is great when you help people choose the right home for their family or get the right price for their home. It's a great feeling to be a true professional who makes buying and selling a pleasurable experience.

- **Don't Lose Contact:** You don't have to be at your client's mercy, but you should stay in communication with them. If your client feels you're constantly MIA or if they can never get in touch with you on urgent matters, they'll assume you don't want to be bothered. This doesn't leave the best impression, and you could potentially miss out on referrals or repeat business. Even if you can't return a phone call within five to ten minutes, make it a goal to return phone calls, emails, and text messages within two to five hours max. Even a brief text or email is better than nothing. You may have five clients or ten clients, but this is the only house they're buying. They are the only client they care about, and you as an agent must respect that reality, even if you're serving several clients in the same time period. Good customer service will also give you personal satisfaction of a job well done.

- **Be Their Advisor:** Buyers and sellers will have questions about the real estate process, the mortgage process, local communities, etc. You can earn their trust and confidence by being their advisor. For this to work, you have to educate yourself on different aspects of the home-buying process. You should be knowledgeable about neighborhoods and local attractions and have basic knowledge about the mortgage process. If you can't answer a question, rather than shrugging it off and moving on to the next topic, offer to do some research or refer your client to someone who can address their concerns - maybe a mortgage broker, a mortgage lender or a home inspector. The reality is, many times as a real estate agent you're also a counselor helping clients work through their fears during potentially one of the most stressful periods of their life. The whole process of searching for a home, agreeing on a price, getting together paperwork, packing, closing the deal, and moving can certainly bring out the best and the worst inpeople.

Remaining Confident in a Down Market

It's easier to be confident when stocks or property prices are going up, but when you read negative news, such as unemployment rates rising or property prices falling, it's easy to lose confidence. In 2007 and 2008, during the great recession, it was quite a shock. My region believed we were immune to real estate fluctuations, as we have an endless number of military buyers and sellers moving every day, literally thousands and thousands per year. However, when the market started to crash, it shocked us all and it happened so fast. Each week it was a bigger falling sky. I will never forget calling my mentor, Larry A., and telling him I'd just bought hundreds of dollars of bullets, flashlights, canned foods, and new guns and that I was thinking I possibly needed to be ready to pack up and drive my family to West Virginia and live in the hills a while. The market was crashing a thousand points per day. My home building partner, Kenton, and I were experiencing huge losses on land we had just bought. If we paid $70,000 for a piece of land, it all of the sudden was only worth $45,000 or less. It was a cash money bloodbath for us, and it hurt. Our stress levels were so high that I would get hives almost daily during that time on my arms and chest. My partner's eyes would turn red, and his vision would blur during part of most weeks. We both had the same local doctor, and it was quite a journey as he tried to fix our illnesses only to find out it was all simply stress and anxiety during that first large period of financial losses in a business venture for me. My partner and I never missed a payment on our bills during that time. We were tremendously creative, and we made deals. We just walked through that season of chaos with one foot in front of the other, scared nearly to death, but we had small children, and financial ruin was not an option we were willing to accept. Below are some tips on remaining confident no matter what the headlines say.

- **Have a Positive Mindset:** With confidence, things seem more achievable. Just like getting into the right mindset for a job interview or overcoming a personal challenge, it's no different growing your real estate wings. Investing your mental energy into a fear mentality can prevent you from finding opportunities, or recovering money from past losses, or even making the right decisions. Some fear is healthy and good, but what you do with the fear is very important. Everyone has a different perspective of risk. Risk tolerance grows just like building your muscles through use and resistance. The more you do it, the more you get used to it. The more you take new steps and try new things, the less fearful you'll be.

The confident or experienced investor may be more comfortable with risk, yet the inexperienced investor may prematurely panic. Know where your limits are so you're able to tolerate market fluctuations. Get into the mindset to accept that prices will fall, but you will not. Develop a mental strategy on how to stay calm and move forward positively. You may need to change the way you do things, adjust who you target, or adjust how you invest your work time, but do not freeze in fear like a deer in headlights.

- **Change Your Focus:** It's a high possibility that, at some point throughout investing, a decision you make won't go as planned. This, of course, can drop your confidence, but don't let your past stop your future progress. By learning from where you went wrong, you can make better decisions and move forward. Accept the consequences of your good and bad decisions. Understand that mistakes or bad decisions can plant a bad seed into your future, and though the fruit is not good, you only truly fail if you don't learn from your mistakes. You may make a $5,000 mistake today, but you may have saved yourself $30,000 in the future. Learning from your imperfect decisions or investments can save you in the long run. Focus on what you can achieve, not what you have not achieved.

- **Think Long Term:** Although people have different ideas about when they want to retire and how much money they need, it's important to have some end goals in mind. A slow and steady approach always wins long term; however, remember to have flexibility for your short-term goals so they can meet the outcomes of the long-term game.

Understanding the Value of the Property as an Agent

As an agent, you need to not only understand the value of what you are selling, but also why. You build your credibility by caring about clients' short and long-term goals. You already have the knowledge of what it takes to be in the business and how it works. You know who to call and where to look for information. The way higher is to know your clients. Clients vary, and they come with different interests, tastes, and lifestyles. As a real estate agent, you know client referrals can be a true golden ticket to earning prospective clients' trust, building your referral network, and ultimately winning new clients. The one small problem? Actually securing new clients and working your referral network is easier said than done! Here are a few thoughts to bear in mind:

- **Know What the Client Wants and Needs:** Determine the type of buyer who would purchase the home you have for sale. Is the home the kind the buyer needs? Does the home fit the parameters of their budget and desire? Is the client single? Are they planning to get married and raise a family in their new home? Do they have kids? How close or far are the schools? You should also consider their age and lifestyle. What public amenities are close by that suit their daily life. Do they like sports? Is that available to them in this area? The list goes on and on, but the point remains the same: Know your client and know what they want. In fact, most clients think of what they want and forget about what they need. It's on you to remind them of the options available to them, including the ones they're forgetting.

- **Are They Working with Another Agent:** We hear stories of buyers calling in a new agent simply because their current realtor has been unreachable for a few hours. This is not always the pushy client's fault. After all, most consumers are not real estate experts themselves, which means they don't always appreciate the ins and outs of agency agreements. Regardless of whether they have signed anything, taking on a client who has committed to someone else can sometimes be a bad idea. Not only might you be stepping directly on your local colleagues' toes, you may also be violating local laws, risking fines and jeopardizing your license. However, it is "America the great," and competition is celebrated and rewarded. If a consumer has an agent they don't like, get released from their buyer/broker contract, and you take them on as a client, can you live with that? Will you feel guilty spending the commission check? The strong survive, and sometimes you have to fight for your daily bread. The choice is up to you. Let your conscience be your guide.

- **Are They Financially Qualified:** This is not just about your bottom line. Asking clients about their financial circumstances is a great way to separate window shoppers from serious buyers. If you're on the buyer side, ask your prospects if they've been pre-approved for a loan. If you're on the seller side, find out how much equity they have in their home. Nevertheless, if a prospective client isn't pre-approved, that doesn't mean you should kick them to the curb. If they seem serious, you can always point them to a lender you trust and who can help you close quickly when the time comes. You, along with a trusted lender, may be able to give these clients advice. Then, you can watch that client follow through on the advice and the check-ins you do. The next thing you know, they send you their friend from work who buys a house, then a neighbor who needs a rental, and then two years later that same renter wants to buy a home. These are not rare miracles, my friend. These can and will happen if you develop the habits of a highly effective real estate agent.

- **What Are Their Expectations:** This goes for everything: their budget, your schedule and availability, the state of the market, the inventory in the area, etc. Many clients will need a little education up front to calibrate their perspective with the facts of the present- day real estate market environment. Realistic benchmarks will save you the trouble of showing them properties they can't afford and will also give you ideas about what areas and homestyles to focus on. If a client continues to ask way too much of you, chances are they won'tbe-come any more cooperative as time goes on.
- **Why Is Now the Right Time to Move:** This question can provide a lot of insight into your client. For one,

some people begin looking for an agent long before they can actually sell, while others wait until the last minute. Asking about timing will let you know how many hours you can expect to work before you can close a sale. Furthermore, the clearer your clients' reasons for moving, the easier the deal will be for you. A client who is pregnant with triplets and presently lives in a small apartment will be far more motivated to do what it takes to close on a home than someone just looking for a change of scenery or to cash out and go into a smaller home that's perfect for retirement.

- **What Have Their Past Experiences Been:** If your clients' previous real estate experience has been positive, you can expect more confidence in your process. If it has been mostly negative, you may have some hurdles to jump in order to earn that trust. On the flip side, this question provides an opportunity to learn from the mistakes of those who've come before you. If a client complains that their last agent didn't communicate well or wasted their time on showings they weren't interested in, you'll know which areas to focus on in building a great working relationship.

Why is My Listing Not Selling?

Once you become an agent and start growing your clientele, you need to know the tips and tricks to ensure your listings sell. You will first need to find the USP, or unique selling proposition, for each home, each community, and each city in which you work. Then, there are four factors that affect the sale of a home: Price, Product, Promotion, and Personnel.

- **Price Analysis**: Is the home priced right? How much are comparable homes in the neighborhood selling for? What are the market times of these comparable homes at those prices? Is your listing at, below, or above market price in comparison to comparable homes? How does the condition of your listing compare to comparable properties? Is it priced according to its condition when comparing or is it too high or too low? Is your listing offering competitive seller concessions in comparison to your competition?

- **Product Analysis**: What are the unique features of this home? What are its challenges? What sets this home apart? Have you identified all the possible buyer objections along with ways to overcome these objections? Overcoming objections may require strategizing preemptively.

- **Promotion Analysis**: Are you highlighting the uniqueness of your listing in all marketing forums? Are you showcasing the value of the home? Are the features of your listing being communicated effectively? How does the home show? Do you drive by and visit weekly if it's vacant? Do you ask real estate agents their opinion of its showing condition? Do you make showing arrangements easy or difficult? Is the home in showroom condition or is it cluttered and unpleasant? Do you have quality photos?

- **Personnel (YOU) Analysis** – After performing all of the above analyses, have you provided your seller with all the necessary information to determine whether the home is maximizing its selling potential? Are you providing proper expectations to your seller? Are you guiding your seller towards necessary action steps to maximize the selling opportunity? Are you giving your seller the necessary feedback about their home and about market conditions?

Becoming and succeeding as a real estate agent can truly be a fun, challenging, and rewarding long-term career. It can serve as a full-time or part-time job, or you can work as a referral-only agent. Succeeding as a real estate agent really comes down to working hard, building momentum, and then leveraging your time through others and technology. If you choose to grow and mature, you will arrive at a place where your schedule becomes more your own. You can go on a vacation and have a strong administrator or agent team members cover for you so that your sales don't slow down while you're gone. You can do transactions on a cell phone or video call with digital signatures as fast as sending or replying to an email. Don't solely judge your real estate success on your first year. Truly embrace the knowledge and experience of every buyer, every seller, every nice home, every eclectic home, and every raggedy, rotten, old home. Take each buyer or seller and teach them, pour into them, but also soak in all the free lessons you're getting in your own life. Whether for your own primary residence or as an investment property, challenge yourself to become a real estate expert and to surround yourself with real estate and business eagles.

CHAPTER 5

PIGS GET FAT, HOGS GET SLAUGHTERED:
KEEPING AND GROWING THE MONEY YOU EARN

During my time as a full-time buyers' agent who focused on new homes, I found my wife had an underlying level of stress because my commissions were up and down. Something came up to jeopardize every single deal. I was always afraid a deal would fall apart. When sales were high, I would just delete a failed deal from my expected income and accept the fact that I had wasted a lot of time. However, when times were lean and my pipeline was low, having to eliminate $5,000 to $40,000 worth of pending transactions was painful and stressful. When I achieved the goal of saving six months of what my family needed to maintain our current lifestyle, it greatly alleviated the quiet stress.

This step I took was very empowering, and it paid me back in huge dividends, not in cash return, but in my confidence in sales and my wife's assurance that we would have a roof over our heads and diapers for our infant son. I can't say in surety I'd do this all again if I had truly understood the cost to my personal life and general enjoyment of my family life. However, I guess I just chose a different path, and once I became 110% committed to growing my companies and succeeding as a conglomerate, I was also committed to not laying off staff when I knew the company needed the staff it had to grow in that next season. Again, leaning into the fear and the chaos. That is the greatest pain and joy of the entrepreneurial journey for me.

Having your finances in order is so important. When your finances are in order, you can more easily enjoy the extras: the new furniture, the vacations, the splurges. If your finances are in disarray, it will negatively affect you in every other aspect of your life. Similarly, if your finances are in good order, every aspect of your life will reap the benefits. This is especially important for agents because even if agents do well professionally but make poor financial decisions, it stresses them out and makes their clients feel like a paycheck. Trust me, the clients can sense this and will often choose a less desperate agent. However, if agents are in a good mental and financial state, it helps them sell easier because they're stronger and more confident. They don't come across as desperate and weak. To put it simply, desperate agents scare clients.

Planning Ahead

For me, looking to the future is natural. Thinking and living and planning five years out is more fun to me than living in my day-to-day duties. That has always been one of my strengths, but Larry A. helped me to embrace that natural gift to see ahead. One of the greatest pieces of advice from him has been the analogy to not just look at the car in front of you; keep your eyes on the horizon and the cars out in front of the immediate cars. If you see a wreck, a lot of red brake lights, or a pack of deer crossing, you can take action quickly and early.

In my undergraduate, I minored in psychology. I loved my classes. One lesson was based on a human study conducted on children they followed for twenty plus years. The students were told by a lab technician that they were going to leave them in the room alone. There was one marshmallow left on the table. They were told they could eat it if they wanted to. However, they were told they could have a second marshmallow later in the day if they did NOT eat the first marshmallow by the time the lab technician came back. The kids sat alone in the room for as long as it took, patiently waiting for the greater reward of two marshmallows instead of just one. The study showed that, twenty years later, the kids who waited for that second marshmallow became more financially successful than the children who didn't wait and impatiently ate the first marshmallow. That lesson has stuck with me ever since. My wife and I reference it around the home and have done so since we were dating. Choosing to wait for the better thing is often a great choice.

There is another family story that comes from my wife's side of the family. My wife's family owned land in rural Philippi, West Virginia, and there was a big coal mining operation buying mineral rights from local farmers and digging for coal there. Each expansion of the coal mining efforts brought the coal company's paychecks closer and closer to her family's land. The other families who sold would frequently celebrate their newfound wealth. So, a common saying around the house was "when the coal comes in." If you need new shoes, we will get some "when the coal comes in." "When the coal comes in," we'll buy one of those new things called a TV. "When the coal comes in," I'll buy you that nicer wedding ring I couldn't afford years ago. Sadly, the coal company went bankrupt and stopped purchasing rights just one farm away from her great-grandfather's land. The coal never came in.

Antithesis means *the opposite of.* If you fail to wait patiently and eat the one marshmallow, you miss out on the big win of two. However, if you wait and delay until the time/money/situation is perfect, you may find later in life that the coal will never come in.

Debt, Loss, and Borrowing Money

I hate debt. I do believe the borrower is a servant/slave to the lender. Debt has cost me much sleep, but it has also helped me ride waves of opportunity that I otherwise would've missed if I wasn't willing to take pretty substantial and scary risks. Please use wisdom. Don't throw your money to the wind, but also don't bury all your money and savings in the sand and accept a tiny interest rate. I recommend having two or three large credit cards of different kinds and charge cards like American Express.

There was a seven-month period where my real estate brokerage company had a combined loss of over $350,000. How did I stomach such a loss? Did I have it piled up in cash and just paid the bills? Boy do I wish that was the case. Unfortunately, that was the second time I needed to come up with such a large sum of money. The first time, I had ninety days to gather about $490,000 due to a new federal government rule called the Dodd Frank Act. The Dodd Frank Act requires a certain amount of cash when starting a joint venture mortgage company. We needed one million dollars. My corporate partner put up their part, and I had to go find my part. How did I come up with that sum of money? My dad didn't give me the money, and I hadn't saved that much money. There was no way around it: I had to borrow money. How did I borrow? When you need to borrow money, where do you start?

- Home equity lines have the cheapest interest rate because they're secured.
- Equity lines on business or rental property are the second cheapest because they're secure, but the interest rates are higher because these properties are not as secure as your home. Banks know that if you come into a difficult financial season, you'll abandon your rental property or office and keep your house last to protect your family.
- Unsecured lines of credit are worth looking into. Wells Fargo, BB&T, and those types of national banks have

some great business deals with unsecured lines of credit. This has helped me make money for many years.

- Business-secured cashflow loans tend to have higher interest rates at approximately 4% to 8% higher than your local bank's unsecured line of credit. These loans are a bit high for my taste. Your daily, weekly, or monthly payments can be really high.

- I typically try to avoid loans from family and friends. My mother and father, on occasion, will make a little loan for an interest rate, or if I find a good deal and they want a good rate of return while we wait for the property to grow in value. However, loans with family and friends can be complicated if expectations are unclear. It is particularly important to document the details of these loans so as not to lead to hard feelings down the road.

Budgeting

The first question to ask when preparing a workable budget is, "How much do I need?" Determine how much money is needed for your annual minimum required expenses. Each person's percentage will be a bit different, but here are some typical norms recommended by experts in the budgeting field. Below is an estimated breakdown of budget percentages that financial advisors often recommend:

- **Anticipated Expenses 40%:** These costs are associated with mortgage/rent payment(s), insurance/healthcare, groceries, vehicle expenses (including insurance, maintenance, monthly payment, and gas), student loans, clothing allowance, household expenses like utilities/ cable, self-care, kids' costs, and pet costs.

- **Taxes 22-33%:** Paying Uncle Sam is inevitable, so count on paying federal and state taxes. Self-employment taxes are a definite possibility as well, unless you plan otherwise and set up an LLC/S-Corp type of business entity.
- **Savings 5%:** Any fiscally sound budget is designed to consistently produce rewards, AKA savings.
- **Investments 17%:** This category is specifically for building a portfolio of performing assets. I typically will use some investment money for really high risk/high reward situations and then another section into more conservative investments that I feel are highly unlikely to lose the initial investment that I make.
- **Luxuries 5%:** Premium cable, exotic vacations, luxury vehicles, regular massages, and fancy dinners are unnecessary. Spend wisely in this area.

There is no need to wait until you've reached your fiscal goals to enjoy the finer things in life. If you don't experience the good things every now and then, you may find it hard to stay on track. Indulge in small extras and understand there are many more around the bend if you stay the course. One of my core beliefs is that those who can live without life's luxuries now are most likely to gain financial freedom in the long run. Walking the balance is a learned practice. It doesn't come overnight.

Saving

Saving is a key component of any budgeting program. Making money is one thing. Holding on to it is another thing entirely. One of the most important reasons to budget is to ensure there is always plenty of money available, even when sales are scarce. Each year, agents must learn how to successfully save for:

- **Taxes:** Determine how much you need to save to pay your taxes (federal, state, and self-employment or business tax) on or ahead of time each year. This is not a good bill to miss payment on since the government can take everything you have now and forever if they decide to come after your back taxes. That was one warning my father gave me time and time again as a young man. Government will reach into your bank account. They will slap liens on all real property, including rentals and homes, if they set their sights on you and have determined you're robbing Uncle Sam. This, my friend, is to be avoided. On the bright side, if you're honest with Uncle Sam and you don't have the money to pay your taxes, they will many times set you up with payment plans and can be very fair in the process. The key is to not stick your head in the sand and think that you won't wake up one day and find your properties are all encumbered with government liens.

- **Unexpected Expenses:** A recommended amount for homeowners to save for home-related expenses is one percent of the home's price each year. If you live in a $300,000 home, then you would put aside $3,000 each year. Other unexpected expenses include deductibles, car repairs, co-pays, and general emergencies.

- **Reserves:** These funds are a backup in case something goes wrong for a short period of time, such as an uncovered illness, sudden job loss, or unexpected move. Experts recommend having at least six to nine months' salary in liquid form for a strong reserve so household costs can be covered without dipping into other funds or borrowing money.

- **Rainy Day Stockpile:** This category can be for anything from true emergencies to impromptu purchases and getaways. It's always good to have a little mad money.

- **Investing:** Putting money into personal investments can be a way to eventually gain financial freedom. Choosing those investments well will make a significant difference in the long term. My friend and business partner, for example, bought a real estate seller-financed note that I brokered him. He paid a minimal amount for it and is still getting payments for it years later. He had some extra fortune when the house for which he owned that seller-financed note ended up being part of a city-wide lawsuit against a large factory for poisoning the soil on the land. That payment itself would have given him his return, not to mention the twelve plus years of payments he also received from it.

- **Vacation/Travel Account:** It's okay to take trips. I think it's very healthy to travel each year. Whether with your family or on your own, you need to step away from your world and from the daily race around the clock.

You need to reset your brain and emotions, and that's the perfect reason to save for them.

- **College Account(s):** Avoid adding to the national student loan debt by saving for post-secondary education funds for your children. Consider using a compounding investment college fund. I set up 529 plans when my children were born, and even when my wife and I have had tighter financial times, we never stopped giving monthly automatically. Fifty dollars each month still adds up. Something is better than nothing. Don't wait until you're financially secure to start saving. That day may never come, but time will keep ticking, and kids will keep growing.

- **Luxury Purchases:** Save for items like luxury cars, expensive presents, extravagant trips, and parties in this category. If there isn't enough money here for what you want, then you may just have to wait. If you can't wait, get creative. Your brain wants to solve problems. Ask yourself, how can I get the $1,400 I need to get this? I don't want to borrow it on a credit card; what do I do? Pay attention. See a great deal on a car a co-worker is selling. Grab it, flip it, and get your $1,400. Take small risks for a big reward. If your risk pays off, get your luxury item. If not, get creative and try again. Maybe take note of unused items around your house. Sell them! Each twenty-dollar sale gets you one step closer to your goal.

Investing

Effective ways to invest include:

- Separate savings accounts
- Financial education
- Index funds
- Certificate of Deposits (CD)
- Annuities
- Money market accounts
- Real estate: seller-financed notes, rental property, storage units, commercial buildings, land, homes, stock and cryptocurrency trading
- Automobiles
- Online sales, such as Ebay
- Your talents: find a creative investment that fits your gifts and network

Most banks want ten to twenty percent down for an investment property unless you're doing an FHA or VA type of loan product. Focus; save up for a down-payment, and start watching for a deal that you can't pass up. The book of Proverbs is full of timeless wisdom. Proverbs 22:7 NIV, says, "The rich rule over the poor, and the borrower is slave to the lender." This verse is still relevant today. When you have debt, especially what is considered bad debt such as high-interest credit cards and car loans, you live in a cycle of always being in the hole. That feeling of always being behind weighs on your mind and causes you to throw money in the trash through high interest.

Allocating Your Income

Take your income into account to get a complete picture of your budget. Allocating percentages may sound all well and good until you enter your specific income into the chart. Using your income makes this exercise real and can really get you thinking about where the money has been going and where it needs to go in the future. Allocating small portions of your income towards things that matter brings a great reward. For example, if $100 is set aside per month from a child's birth, in eighteen years that allotment will equate to $21,600 plus interest, which can be substantial if a good college 529 plan is chosen. You could do the same type of thing for special home projects so that you have small amounts of money growing yearly, and then you could do minor upgrades to your home or yard. It's much easier to come up with $100, $200, or $300 a month than it is to come up with $2,000 or $5,000 in one big after-tax chunk. Think longterm and allocate wisely. Watch your money grow and feel good about your accomplishments. It gives you time to plan as your savings pile up, and many times the project quality is better for the wait in the long run.

Increasing Your Annual Income

After reviewing your budget once income comes into play, you may decide you need more money to live the life you want. Technically, you could make ten dollars more next year, but that probably wouldn't help you achieve your financial goals. Avoid vague objectives. Avoid saying, "I'd like to make more money next year." Instead say, "I want to increase my current sales by ten percent and increase my annual income by at least $10,000." Instead of saying you want more money, say you can increase your current earnings by adding three sales next year. Three sales at $3,333 average net per sale equate to an added

$10,000. Rewording this statement gives you a quantifiable goal that you can work towards and attain.

Agents who can leverage their time using people and technology to avoid burnout will continue to achieve higher income levels. Remember, there's a limit to what you can do in a day. There are only twenty-four hours each day, and without sleep you won't last long. Tired eyes never see a bright future. One way you can leverage your time is to hire quality employees, whether that be a transaction coordinator, a manager, and/or an assistant. If you can get one extra sale each month through leveraging your time, your take-home should increase.

If your end-of-year or projected income seems unfavorable, sit down with your sales manager and work through what can be done to increase your sales income.

At all Simon family companies, we invest substantially when it comes to quality managers who are naturally and authentically passionate about helping our clients attain their goals. We value families. My conglomerate staff, managers, and media team value our agents, and we want them to succeed. If agents' sales are high, but they aren't succeeding in life, then we aren't happy. Our agents are never alone. Moral: Do your due diligence and find a great brokerage to work with.

WORKSHEET 1
DETERMINING EXPECTED EXPENSES

This worksheet may be challenging for many people, but don't get discouraged. Those unfamiliar with this type of activity may find it quite overwhelming at first, but once you begin to chip away at it, the momentum can build, and things will start flowing. After you build the muscle, it becomes easier and easier. Remember, you don't have to complete this task all at once. Break up this worksheet into smaller chunks so that you only spend a couple hours at a time on it and don't get burned out. Consider dedicating a certain block of time each Saturday to this process and then an hour or so after that to maintain it. Many times, a task seems so overwhelming. But, how do you eat an elephant? One bite at a time, my friend. If you make a decent plan and start taking bites from that elephant, you'll quickly find that its size is likely not that of an elephant, and even if your problem is of true elephant size, have faith and start taking bites. You'll be surprised at the positive results. Full mastery will be a big load off, and you'll feel more in control of your finances and your future.

Required tools:
- Last year's itemized expenses—break these up into categories to make it easier
- Complete list of last year's household bills and expenses (mortgage, car loan, utilities, etc.)
- Last year's monthly bank statements
- Last year's statements for credit cards and lines of credit
- Two to three colors of highlighters
- An excel sheet or an accounting program for managing household and self-employment finances; QuickBooks is optimal for LLC or

corporation owners to maintain a merchant account, do payroll, and/or send online invoices.

1. First step is to reconcile. Break down charges for every credit card and line of credit while assigning each charge to fitting expenses for last year's statements. This important step can be very helpful when establishing an overview of your personal finances. Taking the time to ensure this step is done correctly and then maintained as needed can aid in success.

2. Determine last year's annual minimum required expenses for the following:

House Payment/Rent	$ _____
Phone Bill(s)	$ _____
Groceries	$ _____
Clothing	$ _____
Children's Activities/Schools	$ _____
Entertainment/Hobbies	$ _____
Utilities	$ _____
Pest Control	$ _____
Vehicle Costs	$ _____
Dry Cleaning	$ _____
Healthcare/Fitness/Self-Care	$ _____
Other	$ _____

Establish your annual minimum required expenses chart into the budgeting software of your choice or spreadsheet. Then enter your actual information (figures above) into the chart on the next page.

1. Reevaluate each expense once everything has been added to the chart:
   • Ensure all figures in the annual minimum required expenses are indeed *necessary* expenses.

- Make a copy of this worksheet.
- Highlight any nonessential expenses such as lattes, fast food, and impulse online purchases. These types of purchases can become difficult habits to break.
- Use a different color highlighter to highlight any unplanned expenses.
2. Review your annual minimum required expenses from your un-highlighted version. Keep the highlighted copy nearby for later.

You should have arrived at a sum that amounts to your planned annual minimum required expenses, or how much it takes to operate your household each year. This number is the bare minimum you must earn to cover the basic essentials. If this number exceeds that of the household income, expenses must be cut back (letting go of a car, moving into a less expensive home, sending kids to public school instead of private school, etc.), or alternate income growth options need to be taken more seriously.

PLANNED ANNUAL MINIMUM REQUIRED EXPENSES

Household and Family

House Payment/Rent $ _____

Property Taxes $ _____

Property Insurance $ _____

Utilities $ _____

Pest Control $ _____

Security System/Alarm $ _____

Home/Yard Maintenance $ _____

Phone(s) $ _____

Groceries $ _____

Dry Cleaning $ _____

Pet Costs $ _____

Total Household and Family $ _____

Vehicle

Car Payment $ _____

Gasoline $ _____

Maintenance $ _____

Insurance $ _____

Total Vehicle $ _____

Self-Care

Medical/Dental Insurance $ _____

Prescriptions $ _____

Medications/Vitamins/Supplements/Holistic $ _____

Co-Pays $ _____

Massage Therapy $ _____

Chiropractor Visits $ _____

Amazon/Addictive Spurts $ _____

Gym Membership $ _____

Personal Trainer $ _____

Barber/Salon Visits $ _____

Cosmetics/Pesonal Hygiene Products $ _____

Total Self-Care $ _____

Children's School/Activities $ _____

Entertainment/Hobbies $ _____

Grand Total Planned Annual

Minimum Required Expenses $ _____

WORKSHEET 2
ANTICIPATING UNEXPECTED EXPENSES

Fill out the chart below based on what money you can contribute towards unplanned expenses on an annual basis.

Unplanned Annual Minimum Required Expenses

Vehicle Deductibles	$ _____
Vehicle Repairs	$ _____
Medical Insurance Deductibles	$ _____
Medical Uncovered Expenses	$ _____
Household Insurance Deductibles	$ _____
Household Repairs	$ _____
Misc. Emergencies	$ _____
Total Unplanned Annual Minimum Required Expenses	$ _____

Now that you've established what your planned annual minimum required expenses are through previous exercises, you can enter these figures into your budgeting software. The next step is to try to troubleshoot any surprise hits your budget could take. What will be your strategy to plan for emergencies and unforeseen catastrophes in the upcoming year? How can you tuck away some "out of sight, out of mind" cash?

_____

_____

_____

_____

_____

What immediate steps can you take to pad your emergency funds?

_____

_____

_____

What action steps can you take in the next 30 days?

_____

_____

_____

What action steps can you take in the next 90 days?

_____

_____

_____

WORKSHEET 3
SAVINGS AND INVESTMENTS

This form is a basic diagram that can illustrate how much to save. Figure out precise figures by speaking with an accountant and/or financial planner.

Required tools:

- Access to a computer in order to reference your insurance policies
- Last year's bank statements (savings)
- Last year's statements for investments (stocks, college funds, 401k, etc.)
- Calculator

Savings

Not including investments, how much did you save last year? $ _____

How much more money would you like to save this year for:

Taxes? $ _____

Unexpected expenses? $ _____

Reserves? $ _____

A rainy day? $ _____

College account(s)? $ _____

Vacation account? $ _____

Luxury purchases? $ _____

Total amount you want to save this year? $ _____

Investments

Complete the questions below using your investment account statements and compounding table.

Write the total retirement investments you have at this moment. Use the standard 8% if you don't know.

$ _____

Estimate the worth of your current investments upon your retirement.

$ _____

How much yearly return do you expect to earn from your investments?

$ _____

How many years are there until you plan to retire?

$ _____

How much money do you think you'll need for retirement?

$ _____

Multiply your desired annual retirement income by 25. If you will need $80,000 in your retirement, multiply $80,000 by 25 and get $2 million (figure needed to have available through investments at time of retirement).

$ _____

Tally how much you'll need in investment savings each year.

$ _____

Don't be alarmed if the number you need by retirement age seems quite high. The shock that comes along with this number can actually prompt you to make the necessary changes that will result in getting close to or achieving that end result.

WORKSHEET 4
BECOMING DEBT-FREE

How much total debt do you have? Be sure to include home(s), vehicles, student loans, lines of credit and credit cards.

$ _____

What is the total amount of money you spend each month making the effort to pay off the above figures?

$ _____

How much could you increase your worth in 10, 20, 30 years if you allocated the sum of the above two questions towards investments instead of paying to borrow money? Use the standard 8% return.

$ _____

Use the chart below to get a clear view of your credit card debt, so you can begin to understand how paying it off is critical towards becoming financially sound.

Credit Card	Interest Rate	Minimum Payment
1) _____	_____ %	$ _____
2) _____	_____ %	$ _____
3) _____	_____ %	$ _____
4) _____	_____ %	$ _____
5) _____	_____ %	$ _____
6) _____	_____ %	$ _____

1. From highest interest rate to lowest interest rate, list your credit cards in the above diagram. It feels great to pay off each debt and stop the high-interest bleed.
2. List minimum payments for each of these cards.
3. Decide how much money you can pay above the minimum payment every month for the credit card with the smallest balance or highest interest rate and enter that amount.

$ _____

4. Estimate the approximate date this credit card will be paid off by using a credit card calculator; mark the date on a personal calendar.
5. Repeat these above steps until you can see how much and how long it will take to get out of credit card debt. As each credit card is paid off, be sure to add the specific amount of that payment with the collective sum of all credit card payments that precede it.
6. Multiply the overall minimum balance of all your credit cards by 12 (or the number of months left in the year).

$ _____

7. Add the figure from the last question to respective debt payoff section in your budget.
8. Tip: Pay off accounts with high interest rates first or consolidate credit cards into a low-interest term loan. I've utilized transfer balance offers from credit card companies since I was in graduate school. Some of my first real estate investments were with borrowed money with 2%-3% up front at transfer time and then a very low interest rate, typically 3% for 18 months. Considering some creative options like that may help lower your high-interest bleed. Just be careful with the details. The devil is in the details, and it's the little foxes that spoil a grape field. Don't be late on payments.

One late payment could nullify the original interest rate offer and jump to a much higher interest rate. You may also want to stop using the credit card for all other uses. That designated credit card is only where you put debt to pay down faster at a lower interest rate.

Once the above steps are taken, follow through:
- Set up automated pay through your online bank or credit union.
- Resist the urge to increase credit card balances or open new cards/lines of credit with clear intent.
- Stick to this schedule.
- Refrain from fudging or cheating.
- Commit to achieving your goal of being completely debt-free.
- Hire a coach or have a friend hold you accountable.

WORKSHEET 5
BUDGETING FOR LUXURIES

What is the total of your annual minimum required expenses? Include planned as well as unplanned expenses in this figure. $ _____

What amount can you commit to save and invest this year? $ _____

What amount can you specifically use to begin paying off your debt this year? $ _____

Calculate the sum of the above questions. $ _____

What is the total spent on luxury purchases last year? include any monies accounted for in the first three questions. $ _____

How much do you regularly spend on truly unnecessary items? $ _____

Take the above number and multiply it by 52 $ _____

How much would this same money be worth in ten years if it was invested at a 10% return instead of spent? $ _____

Required tools:

- Highlighter
- Every annual expenditure from the complete year
- List of all non-annual minimum required expenses. Use the version that has already been highlighted during the first worksheet.

Directions:

1. Move luxury expenses into appropriate spaces in your budget and highlight it with your marker or colored pen.

2. Look over all your budget expenses. Transfer any expenditures you now feel are luxury items from your annual minimum required expenses into luxury categories.

3. Use the colored highlighter to highlight any expenses that can be considered business expenses. An example would be taking a prospective client to lunch.

4. Add additional luxuries you didn't purchase last year but would like to buy this year.

5. Omit any of last year's luxuries you now feel you can't comfortably afford.

6. Review once again to ensure all expenses are in appropriate sections.

An example of luxury is daily drinking white chocolate mochas at $4.50 each. If you multiply 4 x 7 (days of the week), then take that number (28) and multiply it by 52 (weeks in a year), you get $1,456. Now, take this figure and multiply it by 10% and you get $14,560, which is the amount of money you could have at the end of 10 years if that same money would have been invested instead of spent. That amount is even more astronomical if you calculate compound interest. There were times in my early years I would sacrifice my desires in order to to save a few hundred dollars so I could instead invest it or trade it in the traditional or even penny OTC stock market to try to get a good return. I love taking money and turning it into more money. That, for some reason, makes me feel like a good steward. I ask myself, "How can I be a good steward of this money? Can I take $500 and turn it into $700, or take $50,000 and turn it into $70,000?"

How has your definition of luxury changed during this exercise?

_____

_____

_____

How do you think your new definition will alter future budget-related decisions?

_____

_____

_____

WORKSHEET 6
ALLOCATING YOUR INCOME

How much money do you anticipate earning this year?

$ _____

List how you plan to allocate these earnings and what those percentages equate to in the following categories:

Annual Minimum Required Expenses	% _____	$ _____
Savings	% _____	$ _____
Investments	% _____	$ _____
Debt Pay-Off	% _____	$ _____
Luxuries	% _____	$ _____

If you believe you'll earn enough to afford all of life's expenses, great! No need to worry if you don't think your income will match your financial responsibilities. There are concrete measures that can be taken to make your budget work.

Steps you can take to live on your anticipated income:
- Downsizing to a smaller/less expensive home
- Reducing luxury expenses
- Paying off debt earlier to allow for more wiggle room in the budget
- Conserving household expenses
- Adding supplemental income

Tip: Consider leveraging your time through the use of an assistant, closing coordinator, lead manager, etc. A higher income is often made possible when productivity is increased by delegating busywork.

What would your budget look like if you used the recommended numbers? (See below.)

- Anticipated expenses: 40%
- Taxes: 33% with the new tax plan you may be able to bank on closer to 22%
- Savings: 5%
- Investments: 17%
- Luxuries: 5%

Do you think you're willing to make the necessary changes to live a life you can comfortably afford?

How will you implement these changes?

_____

_____

_____

WORKSHEET 7
INCREASING YOUR ANNUAL INCOME

1. Where am I right now? Am I confident that my numbers are clear and I remembered my primary assets?
2. Which course would I like to commit to over this next season of my life?
3. What actions steps will be required to get there?
4. What is the difference between your current income and the amount you are seeking to earn? $

$ _____

Set realistic and achievable goals that can allow you to increase your income.

_____

_____

_____

Establish what strategies you plan to execute in order to achieve your fiscal goals. List specific work duties you can change/take on that will directly increase your income.

_____

_____

_____

Count the cost of the sacrifices you're considering making.

_____

_____

_____

Set quantifiable time estimates. Record timelines and milestones of your financial journey on your calendar. Review that quarterly. Take a two- to four-day retreat two times a year if you possibly can. Practice planning one to five years out as you build momentum on your dreams and goals. That is revolutionary if you can focus and plan, always keeping yourself on track. Review actual results versus your goals.

Tax Information for Real Estate Agents: Write-Offs

Taxes are a critical component to ensuring your real estate business takes off in the right direction. It can be hard, if not nearly impossible, to correct a tax situation that gets out of hand, which makes it all the more important to track expenses from the get-go. It is the agent's responsibility to understand what expenditures are deductible and to keep a legible record of them. Being a successful real estate agent is not only about creating business, it's also about how well you handle the financial side of your business, and taxes are just one part of that.

Tax write-offs for self-employed agents and/or agents who set up an LLC taxed as an S-Corp for their real estate commissions to be paid to may include, but are not necessarily limited to, the following expenses:

- **A Retirement Plan:** Contributing part of your earnings into a Roth IRA, Keogh, IRA, Simple Employee Pension Plan (SEP), or 401k may allow you to reduce the amount of taxes you're required to pay.
- **Insurance:** Health insurance premiums could be deductible if they aren't paid directly to an employer's health plan(s).
- **Equipment:** When buying office equipment for the purpose of using it in your real estate business, agents may deduct these costs.
- **Self-Employment Tax:** Normally agents are allowed to deduct 50% of the money they pay for this required tax.

- **Home Office:** The IRS now offers a simple way to figure out how to deduct your home office space.
- **Travel:** Typically any form of travel an agent takes while engaging in a business activity can be seen as a deductible expense. Lodging, baggage, and tips may also be covered.
- **Mileage/Vehicle:** Determine which way you'll claim mileage: the standard mileage rate or the actual-cost method. Get the standard mileage rate by calculating the amount of business miles times the current rate per mile allotted by the IRS. The actual cost rate involves taking account of vehicle maintenance, depreciation, car note interest, lease payments (special rules may apply), parking fees, and toll costs.
- **Gifts:** Business gifts that don't cost too much are deductible, as are promotional items or merchandise created to market your business to the general public. Presently, from the advice I've received or read, it's $25 per person per gift, but you need to chat with your CPA to confirm options, as tax laws are continuously changing.
- **Food and Beverages:** Deductible expenses in this category include food, beverages, taxes, tips, meals eaten during business trips, meals provided to employees, transportation to and from restaurants, and foods provided to the public in order to increase business.

Additional Tax Benefits May Include:
- **Being Able to Hire Family Members:** Younger family members can handle minor tasks, and the money paid would be a tax-deductible business expense. For example, fees could be paid to your daughter for making cookies for an open house and your teenager for making flyers for a home you have listed.
- **Credits:** Federal tax credits may be available for you, so check into this to see if you qualify.

Tip: Agents don't have to know about all the tax rules of being self-employed or setting up an LLC and tax structure. They just have to find an accountant who does. There have been agents who've worked hard month after month and who were diligent in paying taxes and played it safe and smart, only to find out later they could have kept more money through tax write-offs each year. For example, saving and/or keeping rather than paying Uncle Sam just $3,000 a year could be that needed vacation, a chunk towards a down payment on a small rental property, fun money, or possibly even a couple of mortgage payments. Accurately tracking client meals, business gifts, company brand logo clothing, health insurance, retirement accounts, car mileage, and continuing education costs will help you keep more of your hard-earned money. "Pigs get fat. Hogs get slaughtered." Do all you can to pay only what you're required to pay, but don't be a hog and try to trick Uncle Sam. If you lie on your taxes, you may get slaughtered.

Keep Tax Records by Noting:
- The amount of money spent
- Type of business activity done during this activity
- Exact time, date, and place.
- Names of individuals involved
- Per Diem (if applicable)

Note: For more information about self-employment taxes, check with your CPA or visit http://www.irs.gov/Individuals/Self-Employed.

CLOSING

My greatest success thus far in life, and my greatest dream come true, is my family—remaining faithful and committed to my wife and investing my energies into loving my two children. I'm thankful for Jami chasing me to Virginia (my version, anyways) a year and a half after I left to "further her career near someone she knew and maybe kissed on occasion," (her version). In my early years, I hungered greatly for a spouse with whom I could hold close at night and share my life. I wanted mutual love, trust, and shared values. Jami is that woman I hope to grow old with. My children, Ethan and Ella, are my greatest investment, specifically spending time with them, speaking into their lives, challenging them, and pushing them to work hard, try hard, dream, and set goals. That is my true mission for my 40s. No pressure. There may be chaos, and there may be hard times, but in the end, I have hope and faith that my children will ultimately make good choices, sow good seeds, and make a great impact on the lives of others while they walk this earth on their own human journey.

If by the time you read this book and all of my companies are closed, shut down, and dust and rust has destroyed what remains, whether through my own errors in judgment, through a future unexpected great depression or a war, a flood, a fire from the sky, whatever the reason, it's not the goal in the end that matters. It is not the end result. The desired thing, really and truly, is about the journey—the human journey of walking with co-workers, family, and friends through the ups and downs of our lives. Sometimes tragedy awaits us and those we love along the way. Embrace the day and the journey of each week. You don't know when your last breath will be and when you'll return to dust. If you only can be happy when you get rich, get married, get a car or get a business, then, my friend, you will never truly be happy. Walking in peace and joy regardless of your circumstances is really what this is all about.

When I was a kid, I had a friend from the church who saw an older lady in a broken-down car stuck on a railroad track. He went to try to help push the car out of the way. He was not trying to save a life, just simply moving the car. He turned and saw a train coming down the track toward him. I remember hearing it described that he just froze in fear and was struck and killed by the train. That is a true story, and he's certainly not the first person who has died because of his response, or lack thereof, to fear. Year over year, I'd see his father and brother continue to faithfully attend church. It broke my heart and it always stuck with me. Freezing in fear can be a very human natural response, but we must challenge ourselves to react, respond, and take strong action. Fear is something I've struggled with my entire life, including fear of failure and fear of success. They have both been true battles that I've fought throughout my life. My staff sometimes thinks I act too quickly on some matters and too slowly on others. I just do the best I can and take it one day and one week at a time.

Don't let fear keep you from chasing your dreams and goals, whatever they may be. Obviously, I think some of the biggest dreams can be accomplished through real estate, whether that's buying your own house, buying property to build your business on, or deciding to help others find and buy their dream home or property. If real estate is included in your dreams, I would be honored to help you accomplish them.

POSITIVE AFFIRMATIONS

- I dare to boldly stay true to my dreams and not allow every thought that floats through my head, nor my emotions, stop me from dreaming, planning, and acting on my goals and dreams.
- I dare to feed excitement to my mind, my body, and my emotions daily, weekly, and yearly. Today I will take action on good habits that will build a good future.
- I dare to push through the emotions and pain of walking through what feels like chaos as I battle to achieve my dreams and goals. Fear will not control me. I will do it afraid!
- My goals and dreams are mine. Because they are mine, I give myself permission to write them with pencil and not pen. I give myself permission to adjust my dreams and goals as I grow and mature.

- I will no longer blame my failures on my family, friends, or those who have hurt me and held me back. I am the only one to answer for my life. The past is the past and I must turn from the mistakes of the past and focus on planting good seeds into my future daily, and with neverending, yet balanced, efforts. I will embrace my lessons and learn from my highs and my lows.
- Activity Does Not Equal Productivity, I will focus on productivity.
- Today, regardless of the setbacks and unmet expectations, I will, at my core, hold to a Hopeful Expectation of Good.
- I dare to dream of a new season of my life. Seasons change, and so must I.

ABOUT THE AUTHOR

Dr. Brian P. Simon, a West Virginia native turned Hampton Roads, Virginia resident, is an avid entrepreneur who credits his many accomplishments to surrounding himself with likeminded, driven individuals. He first came to Hampton Roads with the hope of making a significant impact on as many people as possible, but not exactly sure how he would do that and never expecting that his greatest impact would be in the real estate industry. He obtained his doctoral degree from Regent University and is the founder of several successful real estate-related companies, primarily Fit Realty. He specializes in land acquisition, new construction, and real estate marketing and advertising with more than fifteen years' experience in internet and social marketing strategies. Brian's greatest professional enjoyment comes from training, equipping, and empowering agents, employees, and partners to succeed.

Although an entrepreneurial spirit by nature, Dr. Simon's greatest passion is his family. He enjoys fishing with his son, hunting, gatherings with friends, and lock-down Netflix binges with his wife. He also thoroughly enjoys staying current on the latest technology.

Brian resides in Suffolk, Virginia with his family.

RESOURCES

The Brian Simon real estate team, which we ran under the banner of SimonHouses.com from those early days, and now our growing boutique brokerage Fit Realty and our growing real estate and home builder CRM Lead Ignite, has sold over $800,000,000 in real estate in the last twelve years.

Vision

To be the change in real estate that creates a culture of success through individuals grounded in our core values.

Mission

Provide diversified real estate business developmental growth solutions to create success and stability regardless of market conditions.

Core Values

Commitment to Others

The act of engaging ourselves daily to each other in trust and encouragement enriching the lives around us

Active Learning

To gain positive habits by experience and exposure by example.

Human Dignity

Mutual recognition of personal value with honoring the inherent value in all persons; to live and act in a manner of higher ethical standards, especially under pressure

InteGRITy-Based Perseverance

Strength of moral character that results in; courage and resolve; perseverance with passion

At Lead Ignite, we help you capture real estate leads. We send you reminders to keep you up to date with all of your clients. We help you close deals because our transaction management features make communicating with all the right people easy. Thus, agents are able to work more efficiently, accomplishing more in a shorter amount of time with the ability to repeat this process more often. Lead ignite helps our agents grow their traditional grass roots real estate business, as well as makes online and social lead generation and conversion a seamless process.

FitCoin is our real estate referral company, which works to serve agents who are either no longer actively selling yet wish to create a stream of income simply by using their license for referrals, or who are new to real estate and wish to slowly grow their business. At FitCoin, we give our referral agents an account in Lead Ignite, as well as a website platform and access to our library of trainings developed to help you grow in knowledge and to stay current. FitCoin referral agents get paid every time one of their referrals results in a closing.

*****

Custom Homes of Virginia is my home building company with my faithful and loyal partner, Kenton McClung, who is a Class A builder, as well as president and manager of the company.

Custom Homes of Virginia has built or renovated and re-sold over 300 homes in the last ten years. At CHOV, we understand that revitalizing and tearing down the old and building the new is all part of the reshaping and rebuilding of America and keeping the streets and homes safe and clean. Renovating or tearing down old homes brings us joy. At CHOV, we find great satisfaction building new homes in older neighborhoods. Old, dilapidated homes have been torn down, and now the streets are lined with our gorgeous homes.

Land Lovers is our land-holding company, also owned by me and my partner, Kenton. This company was created based on the belief that land is the core of all home building, and we believe in the common statement that "a builder is only as good as his land." Since 2008 we have invested in land technology, and thus it only made sense for us to establish our own land-holding company.

BriK is our home renovation company. At BriK, we believe your home should reflect your style and needs while complimenting your personality. We can take a one hundred-year-old, dilapidated home and turn it into your dream home. Creating a truly custom home is our passion. Even the smallest details are important. Our staff designer has experience in helping clients bring their vision to life. Our selections surpass industry standards, giving our clients many options from which to choose.

*****

My title company, Leader's Title, is a partnership with a local attorney, L.T. Caplan. We have closed thousands of titles in the last eight years in that entity. We are a full-service title company serving clients throughout Virginia and beyond. We specialize in purchase and sale agreements, as well as REO and short sale closings. We are proficient in representing both buyers and sellers either in-house or in the client's location of choice within the United States. We can acquire titles by multiple underwriters. We ensure quick turnaround times for title binders and even less time for refinances. We are able to schedule remote closings and accommodate last minute closings. We also obtain payoff, offer competitive pricing, and prepare HUD-1 settlement statements. At Leaders Title, LLC, we believe in going above and beyond when it comes to putting our clients first.

*****

SIMON STUDIOS

Simon Studios is my full-service branding studio with my partner, Ethel Delacruz. The company is dedicated to creating clean, crisp, consistent work for your brand identity. In a world overflowing with content, our goal is to make yours stand out and what sets us apart from other agencies is that we're made up of specialized studios—including film, graphic and interactive design, marketing, and music—from which your brand will receive customized treatment. In the last three years, we have grown from nothing to a solid client list. Visit www.simonstudios.com to see our accounts. We are just beginning! The talent and giftedness abound in this company.

*****

Simon.Mortgage

Partnering with a trusted mortgage company is an essential cornerstone to serving clients in the realm of residential real estate, which is why we created a mortgage resource center, Simon.Mortgage. Residential home buyers need tremendous protection, and knowledge is how good decisions are made. At Simon.Mortgage, we can help you make informed decisions and refer you to the right people when it comes time to find the appropriate loan for your needs.

Mortgages are essential in residential, commercial and land purchases, both for private ownership and for investment property. Our family of companies has closed over $500,000,000 in residential mortgages. Our affiliated loan officers have earned many awards in Virginia, including the top one percent Originators, VHDA Top Producing Loan Officers, Best VA Lenders (Scotsman Guide), and, for eleven consecutive years, the Chairman's Club Award. They also have accumulated awards in other states, including Top Originator in the Nation for VA Loans (Scotsman Guide).